HADRIAN VII

HADRIAN VII

A PLAY BY PETER LUKE

WITH AN INTRODUCTION BY HERBERT WEINSTOCK

BASED ON HADRIAN THE SEVENTH AND OTHER
WORKS BY FREDERICK ROLFE, "BARON CORVO"

NEW YORK ALFRED A. KNOPF 1969

INTRODUCTION

Peter Luke's *Hadrian VII* was first staged on May 9, 1967, by the Birmingham (England) Repertory Theatre in association with Bill Freedman and Charles Kasher; Alec Mc-Cowen acted the role of Fr. William Rolfe–Hadrian VII. That production was taken to London, where it opened at the Mermaid Theatre on April 18, 1968, becoming a prolonged success. Mr. Luke's play is based closely upon selected incidents in the known life of "Frederick Baron Corvo"—that is, Frederick William Rolfe—and upon his writings, chiefly his novel *Hadrian the Seventh*. Like all plays based upon novels and/or biographies, it naturally is selective rather than inclusive. For that reason, some information about both Rolfe and *Hadrian the Seventh* and his other publications can be a useful background against which to approach the play.

The man whose full name was (or perhaps just should have been) Frederick William Serafino Austin Lewis Mary Rolfe was born to middle-class Broad Church Anglican parents in London on July 22, 1860. He left school, and then home, at the age of fifteen; he died in Venetian squalor on October 25, 1913. Between 1875 and his death, he zigzagged through a life to which the adjective "checkered" would attribute a regularity that it never approached. He sometimes taught ordinary subjects peculiarly to baffled students in

English lay and Catholic schools; alternately coddled and quarreled with his acquired Roman Catholicism; wrote gnomic, wrongheaded pamphlets and brilliant but often obscure books; did ghostwriting; failed in persistent, long-drawn-out attempts to become a priest; painted; invented; composed. One of his paintings depicted the translation of St. William of Norwich, a twelfth-century boy martyr of twelve with whom he had fallen in self-identifying love. Characteristically, the one hundred and forty-nine priests and other attendants displayed in gorgeous vestments all revealed Rolfe's own face; so, as if to make the point conclusive, did the body of the dead Saint. Recognizing his own weakness as a figure painter, Rolfe usually photographed a model, made a lantern slide of the photograph, and then projected the figure onto the area to be painted, where he sketched in its outlines. A. J. A. Symons, his fascinated biographer, reported that some of Rolfe's oils were "enhanced with needlework and spangled with sequins."

Figuratively at first, but then in reality, Rolfe took the road to Rome. And after his Italianization had set in, his vagabondage became so intricate, covert, indigent, and complex, so crowded with hidden and perhaps unmentionable incident, that Symons's attempt to recover it all but baffled him. Rolfe somehow persuaded an Englishwoman who had become *la duchessa* Carolina Sforza-Cesarini to support him for some time; he later asserted that by transferring to him certain properties in Italy she had given him the right to a baronial title. He played the piano, composed music, dabbled in deep-sea and other photography,[1] wrote triolets, designed

[1] A remarkably prescient digression in *Hadrian the Seventh* foretold modern color photography and even appears to have outlined some of its procedures. Rolfe actually and fruitlessly patented devices for color and submarine photography—he was a splendid swimmer—and for magnesium-flash lighting.

furniture and typography, lived—as Symons wrote—"on his wits and the means of others." As a suppliant, he was almost always aggrieved and litigious, almost never grateful.

Once Rolfe suggested that he be declared mentally unbalanced so that he might escape constant abject poverty in the free lodging and meals of an asylum. In 1898, he was mercilessly, gratuitously attacked in the *Aberdeen Free Press* —he had for a time been on the rolls of the Aberdeen Association for the Improvement of the Poor. At another juncture, he was being paid eighteenpence each for preparing reports of inquests. Near the end, his hair dyed an unlikely red, he plied a silk-sailed, vividly painted *sandalo* on Venice's canals and surrounding waters.

As Sir Shane Leslie wrote of Rolfe: "In the curious game of applying fictitious parentage he might have been placed as a fiery cross between Gilles de Retz and Marie Bashkirtseff." The late A. J. A. Symons's compulsive, persistent effort to solve the rebuses of Rolfe's life resulted, in 1934, in the publication of his *The Quest for Corvo*. That surpassing book contains all that Symons could learn and felt able to repeat. From its pages rises a human being as peculiar and heroic and dingy and nearly demonic as the fictitious Pope Hadrian himself. In it, as in the pseudonymous portraits of himself with which Rolfe-Corvo's other books are crowded, his half-revealed homosexuality provokes a special, unmistakable atmosphere—which, when joined, as in *Hadrian the Seventh*, with his bewitched adoration of the panoply, rulings, and ritual of Roman Catholicism, produced a masterpiece— minor, but still a masterpiece.

Rolfe first attracted attention as a writer in 1895–6, with six tales published in the *Yellow Book;* these were reissued in volume form by John Lane in 1898 as *Stories Toto Told Me,* one of the Bodley Booklets, of which another was

Max Beerbohm's *The Happy Hypocrite*. The colophon of Rolfe's first book is such characteristic Rolfe-Corvo as to be worth rescuing. It reads:

> Thus ended the sixth of the nine and forty stories Toto told me: wherein have been contained high and great matters concerning the noble army of martyrs and all the company of heaven with other divers legends histories and acts as all along hereafore is made mention, which works I have so far written down at the commandment and request of my special patron John Lane and have finished at Corvicastra in Aria² on the Feast of the good thief Saint Dismas the year of our Lord *m viic xc viii* and the *lxi* of the reign of Queen Victoria. By me Baron Corvo. Printed for John Lane by John Wilson and Son at the University Press, Cambridge, Mass.

In 1901 was issued the earliest of Rolfe's books to have survived in the sense of having been made available later in a modern edition. *In His Own Image* as republished by John Lane in 1924 contains fourteen of the Toto-told stories headed "Spring" and numbered, with essential Rolfian finicalness, I, IJ, IIJ, and up to XIJ, which is followed by α and β; then come twelve stories headed "Summer" and numbered from XIIJ to XXIIIJ; and, finally, there are the six stories from the 1895–6 *Yellow Book*, the original *Stories Toto Told Me*. The volume is dated "From London, in my study, on the eve of Saint George the Martyr, Protector of the Kingdom, MDCCCC," and is dedicated "DIVO AMICO DESIDERATISSIMO D. D. D. FRIDERICUS."

---

² Rolfe apparently intended this castle in the air to be taken as the seat baronial of the imaginary Corvos. For his next book, he designed the Corvo coat of arms, which Sir Shane Leslie described as "a Raven for Corvo sable on argent, a lapel of three and a cross potent on a field—argent and sable countercharged, surmounted by a Hat Priestly sable for crest and surrounded for motto by the Greek ΕΣΤΑΙ ΠΑΝΤΑ ΚΑΛΩΣ (All will be well)."

In 1901, Grant Richards published Rolfe's learned, prickly, lopsided paean of praise to Alexander VI and wholly remarkable rehabilitation of Cesare and other Borgias. This *Chronicles of the House of Borgia* has been reissued several times.[3] It can repay the most careful attention from readers not liable to make the mistake of thinking it trustworthy biography or faithful history. What appears to have been Rolfe's next publication came from the Bodley Head in 1903: *The Rubaiyat of Umar Khaiyam* "done into English from the French of J. B. Nicholas by Frederick Baron Corvo." This peculiar volume carried the French text by Nicolas (not Nicholas),[4] as well as an Introduction by the prolix American editor, writer, and Omar-enthusiast Nathan Haskell Dole.[5] Those who might savor something of what Rolfe made of Omar may—with both FitzGerald and certain homosexual references in mind—contemplate his rendering of the opening quatrain of the *Rubáiyát:* "Lo Phosphor! And a voice from the Tavern crieth: Enter, hilarious Philopots, hybrist Youths; enter and fill yet one more Cup of Wine before that Fate shall fill brimful your Cup of Life."

Now dropping his Corvine disguise, Rolfe next published (Chatto and Windus, London, 1904) *Hadrian the Seventh* under his real name: this was issued in the United

[3] In 1931, Random House reissued it in New York, in the Modern Library, under the title *A History of the Borgias*. That edition carried the Introduction by Shane Leslie, which already had appeared in Alfred A. Knopf's reissue of *In His Own Image*.

[4] Louis-Jean-Baptiste Nicolas (1814–75), an interpreter in the French diplomatic service and a student of Oriental languages, had translated what was then thought to be the entire body of poetry attributed to Omar, not merely the selection from it made use of by FitzGerald.

[5] John Lane also issued (1924) this translation of 464 quatrains in another edition, with sixteen "Persian" colored illustrations by Hamzeh Carr. That edition carries an Introduction by Edward Heron-Allen, F.R.S., who also edited it "with notes and a comparative study of the original texts." This time it was carefully, diacritically entitled *The Rubáiyat of 'Umar Khaiyám*.

States in 1925 by Alfred A. Knopf.[6] It contains the extraordinarily inappropriate dedication "To Mother"—Mrs. Rolfe is prominent chiefly by her absence from biographical accounts of her son—a formula of obedience to a decree of Urban VIII, a long "Prooimion," and the twenty-four dazzling chapters of the novel's text.

It was also Chatto and Windus, London, who published (1905) Rolfe's *Don Tarquinio*. Subtitled "A Kataleptic Phantasmatic Romance by Fr.[7] Rolfe" and dedicated to the author's brother Herbert Rolfe, *Don Tarquinio* describes one day in the very active and questionable life of a young, handsome late-fifteenth-century noble attached to the House of Borgia. Apparently the last of Rolfe's books to be issued while he lived was brought out by William Rider and Son, London, in 1912: *The Weird of the Wanderer,* "being the Papyrus records of some incidents in one of the previous lives of Mr. Nicholas Crabbe [Rolfe]. Here produced by Prospero and Caliban." This was an unequal collaboration with a large, wealthy young man called Harry Pirie-Gordon, whose family long befriended and supported Rolfe, and whom Rolfe had nicknamed Caliban (he himself being Prospero) with reference to his having taught Pirie-Gordon to "speak"—that is, to write. Pirie-Gordon did indeed publish one or more books over his own name. *The Weird of the Wanderer,* despite some passages in uncorrupted Rolfean prose, is the poorest of the books published by Rolfe during his lifetime.

Unpublished when Rolfe died in 1913 (or, if published, then received in unrippled silence) were at least five other books, not to mention another but aborted collaboration with Pirie-Gordon. The five were: *Don Renato, an Ideal Content,*

---

6 And reissued by him in 1953 with an Introduction by the present writer.
7 Having abandoned Corvicastra in Aria, Rolfe undoubtedly hoped that this "Fr[ederick]" would be misread as Fr[ater], and thus would help to establish his ecclesiastical, as distinct from his baronial, masquerade.

the purported diary of an early-sixteenth-century priest at
Rome (issued by Chatto and Windus with an Introduction
by Cecil Woolf in 1963); a translation with Sholto Douglas,
The Songs of Meleagros of Gadara (unpublished); *Hubert's
Arthur*, a novel of the era of King John which was still another "collaboration" with Pirie-Gordon (published in 1953
as edited by A. J. A. Symons); *The Desire and Pursuit of
the Whole*, a "Romance of Modern Venice" which retails
more of the life of Nicholas Crabbe (Rolfe), this time as
involved in the Messina earthquake of 1908 and with a
psychically hermaphroditic hero-heroine inelegantly named
Zildo (New Directions, New York, 1953, with a Foreword
by W. H. Auden; Chatto and Windus, London, 1958); and
Nicholas Crabbe, or The One and the Many, which Symons
described as standing "midway between *Hadrian the Seventh*
and *The Desire and Pursuit of the Whole* in the autobio-
graphical trilogy wherein Rolfe recorded his adult life" (New
Directions, New York, with an Introduction by Cecil Woolf,
1958; Chatto and Windus, London, 1958, with "an appendix
of letters from Sholto Douglas to Rolfe").[8]

Many of Rolfe's publications are only for enthusiasts,

---

[8] In 1957, Nicholas Vane, London, issued in a limited edition the posthumous
collection of Rolfe stories entitled *The Cardinal Prefect of Propaganda
and Other Stories*, with an Introduction by Cecil Woolf. *Three Tales of
Venice* (Corvine Press, Thames Ditton, England, 1950) had consisted
of stories by Rolfe originally published in *Blackwood's Magazine*. No
collected edition of Rolfe's letters has been issued, but the following
selections all contain what Rolfe would have called "high matters":
*Letters to C. H. C. Pirie-Gordon, edited with an Introduction by Cecil
Woolf and an Epilogue by Caliban*, a limited edition, Dufour Editions,
Chester Springs, Pennsylvania; *Letters to R. M. Dawkins, edited with
an Introduction by Cecil Woolf and an Epilogue by Laura M. Ragg*,
a limited edition, Nicholas Vane, London; *Letters to Leonard Moore,
edited with an Introduction by Cecil Woolf and Bertram W. Korn and
an Epilogue by Leonard Moore*, a limited edition, Nicholas Vane, London.
Cecil Woolf also compiled *A Bibliography of Frederick Rolfe, Baron
Corvo* (Essential Books, Fair Lawn, New Jersey, 1957).

who are not few; but his enduring reputation depends upon *Hadrian the Seventh*. A novel that is a cry for mercy, a wishful and covert autobiography never intended to be taken literally, *Hadrian the Seventh*, like most of Rolfe's other fictions, is a *roman à clef* wildly and often ferally unjust to several of his onetime friends and enemies. It tells of an early-twentieth-century Briton who is borne up with stunning suddenness from snarling penury and obscurity to the Throne of St. Peter. This hero, called George Arthur Rose,[9] both ascetic and epicene, shows himself both wise and naïve. He selects his pontifical style because, as he says: "The previous English pontiff was Hadrian the Fourth;[1] the present English pontiff is Hadrian the Seventh. It pleases Us; and so, by Our Own Impulse, we command."

Thus Rose-Hadrian-Rolfe-Corvo defies the cardinals who want him to be a Leo, a Pius, or a Gregory (this is a scene of high comedy in Mr. Luke's play)—and a very English Hadrian, in the finest line of English eccentrics, he becomes. Preparing an evening-length play, Mr. Luke obviously could not make use of many of the novel's teeming situations and scenes; he well concentrates on those which can make for continuous dramatic-theatrical development. Thus, he does not include Rose-Hadrian's immediate determination to deal conclusively with the secular affairs of nations. Hadrian advances grandly into international diplomacy. Rolfe composed the Pope's history in the dawn of our century, and powerful personages of that era appear in it *in*

---

9 In *Hadrian VII*, he is Fr. William Rolfe until he becomes Pope; but thereafter a young seminarian appears who is named George Arthur Rose— and he too represents one of Rolfe's Protean changes.

1 Nicholas Breakspear, styled Hadrian (Adrian) IV, was Pope from 1154 to 1159. During the first year of his reign, he gave Ireland to Henry II, King of England. No other Englishman ever became Pope.

propria persona. If Wilhelm II and Victor Emmanuel III,[2] who move across the novel's brocaded pages to its end, be judged by what ensuing decades made of them, Rolfe must be called a poor prophet. But intermittently he was a seer: in *Hadrian the Seventh* he foresaw not only the Russian Revolution of 1917, but even the murder of Nicholas II, the Tsarina, and their children. Still, the secular pseudohistory in his novel (it does not appear in the play) is the merest game, however intently Rolfe played at it. Rolfe's raging antisocialism and some of his other inhumane tenets can be repulsive when they are not merely silly; they matter even less than his pseudohistory.

What matters in *Hadrian the Seventh* is George Arthur Rose himself. What matters is the robes and jewels he as Pope wears and beholds, the splendid words he uses and invents, his astonishing accesses of venom and love, his daily life at the center of the spacious pageant of the Vatican— "the dim light where motionless forms of Cardinals curved like the frozen crests of waves carven in white jade and old ivory on a sea of amethysts . . ." What matters most is a novelist capable of imagining both the scenes that Mr. Luke has adapted so expertly in his remarkable play and some that he had to leave unused—as, for example, the confrontation during which the Pope is conquered for love by the infant Italian prince and princess or the scene in which Hadrian, supported on one hand by the Northern Emperor and on the other by the Southern, is assassinated near the tomb of Hadrian the Emperor: "The Apostle raised himself a little, supported by imperial hands. How bright the sunlight was,

[2] Rolfe once broadly hinted that Kaiser Wilhelm had been his godfather. As for the Italian king, whom he greatly admired, he elaborated a genealogy demonstrating that little Victor Emmanuel was the rightful king of England—and thereafter always sent presentation copies of his new books to the royal residence in Rome.

on the warm grey stones, on the ripe Roman skins, on vermilion and lavender and blue and ermine and green and gold, on the indecent grotesque blackness of two blotches, on apostolic whiteness and the rose of blood."

Graham Greene once said of *Hadrian the Seventh* that "it is a novel of genius, standing in relation to the other novels of its day much as *The Hound of Heaven* stands in relation to the verse"—and certainly that comparison is just in the matter of fervor and high purpose. And it was D. H. Lawrence (one is mightily tempted to say "of all people!") who wrote of Rolfe's masterpiece: "The book remains a clear and definite book of our epoch, not to be swept aside. If it is the book of a demon as his contemporaries said, it is the book of a man demon, not a mere poseur. And if some of it is caviare, at least it came out of the belly of a live fish." And so it did. Peter Luke's success is measured by the high degree of his achievement in transferring to the very different medium of the spoken stage some of the qualities rather than all of the letter of *Hadrian the Seventh*.

"Pray for the repose of His soul. He was so tired."

Herbert Weinstock

HADRIAN VII

CHARACTERS

Fr. William Rolfe

Mrs. Crowe

First Bailiff

Second Bailiff

Agnes

Dr. Talacryn,
Bishop of Caerleon

Dr. Courtleigh,
Cardinal-Archbishop of Pimlico

Jeremiah Sant

The Cardinal-Archdeacon

Father St. Albans,
Prepositor-General of the Jesuits

Cardinal Berstein

Cardinal Ragna

Rector of St. Andrew's College

George Arthur Rose

Papal Chamberlains

Cardinals

Seminarists

Papal Guards

Swiss Guards

Acolytes

A NOTE ON THE APPEARANCE AND BEHAVIOURISMS OF
ROLFE / HADRIAN

*Frederick William Rolfe, when the play opens, is a
smallish, spare man, of about forty. He wears his grey-
ing hair very short, is myopic and can hardly see without his plain, steel-rimmed spectacles, but he is slim,
agile and erect.*

*His tastes are austere but he is fond of such things as
goat's milk, apples, raw carrots, fresh linen and particularly water, both to drink and to wash in. He is a
practical man and carries a penknife with which he pre-
pares his apples, sharpens pencils, etc.*

*He smokes a lot, always rolling his own and tucking
the ends in with a pencil. Cat-like, his movements are
swift, lithe and silent. Likewise, there are moments
when he remains utterly still. As Pope, he comports
himself with extraordinary dignity when the occasion
demands, though "off-duty" he reverts to his more abnormal self. In the early part of Act I and at the end of
the play, Rolfe wears a threadbare clerical grey suit.
During the rest of the play, Rolfe/Hadrian wears such
canonical dress as may be appropriate.*

ACT ONE

SCENE ONE

A corner of FREDERICK ROLFE's *bed-sitting room in London.*
*The room is the abode of a poor scholar of fastidious
habits and austere tastes. There is a small gas-fire R, the
meter for which is on the wall down R. Up L is the door
leading to the rest of the house. A small chest-of-drawers is
up C, and below it a wooden armchair. Religious painting
covers the walls, and there is a small crucifix on the wall
below the fire. Next to the gas meter is a mirror. A wooden
chair is wedged beneath the door-handle. Books lie around,
and there is a bottle of ink on the floor below the armchair.*
When the curtain rises, ROLFE *is seated in the armchair
writing a manuscript on his knees, and smoking a fat, untidy
rolled cigarette which he seldom takes out of his mouth. He
is shivering with cold, and has a blanket wrapped around
him. After a moment there is a knock on the door.* ROLFE
*looks round to make sure the chair is firmly wedged in place
and smirks with satisfaction. The knocking is repeated more
peremptorily, accompanied by rattlings of the door-handle.*

MRS. CROWE *(off)* Mr. Rolfe. *(She tries the handle, which
does not give.)* Mr. Rolfe! *(She rattles the handle.)* What's
the matter with this door? Mr. Rolfe, I know you're there.

7

ROLFE   Tickle your ass with a feather.

MRS. CROWE *(off)*   What did you say?

ROLFE   Particularly nasty weather, Mrs. Crowe.

MRS. CROWE *(off)*   Mr. Rolfe, I haven't climbed all these stairs just to be insulted. There are two gentlemen below who wish to see you.

ROLFE *(starting up; noticeably startled)*   To see *me?*

MRS. CROWE *(off)*   Yes, to see you.

> *(ROLFE quickly takes the fag-end out of his mouth and moves to the door to remove the barricade. MRS. CROWE enters furiously. She is a widow of about forty with pretentions to good looks and gentility. She succeeds only in being "genteel." ROLFE looks nervously past her down the staircase.)*

MRS. CROWE   Ah, I thought you'd come off your high horse when you heard that.

ROLFE *(recovering slightly)*   Oh—well, I'm very busy.

> *(He puts the chair L of the door.)*

MRS. CROWE   They said it was a private matter which couldn't wait.

ROLFE *(attempting to bluster)*   I'm not prepared to see them unless they state the precise nature of their business, Mrs. Crowe.

MRS. CROWE   If you think I'm going to run all the way up and down these stairs like a skivvy to carry your messages . . . *(Significantly)* I think you'd better see them, Mr. Rolfe.

ROLFE   Oh? Hmmmm! Very well. Please show them up, Mrs. Crowe, but let it be understood—

(MRS. CROWE *exits, shutting the door.*)

ROLFE   —that I haven't got all day. *(Crossing to the mirror)* Lascivious bitch! *(He quickly takes a stiff white collar and a plain black tie from the chest-of-drawers and puts them on. He hastily puts a packet of oatmeal out of sight in a drawer, then sits and makes notes on his manuscript.)* I'm in an awful state. Calm down, calm down, buck up. *(Hearing footsteps)* Oh, my God . . .

(There is the sound of footsteps mounting the stairs, and with a peremptory knock . . .)

ROLFE   Come in.

(. . . MRS. CROWE ushers in the two BAILIFFS. The SECOND BAILIFF is a venerable-looking old man with white hair. His colleague, the FIRST BAILIFF, is a tall, amiable, healthy-looking fellow in his early forties. It is suggested that they should bear a resemblance to DR. COURTLEIGH, Cardinal-Archbishop of Pimlico, and DR. TALACRYN, Bishop of Caerleon, respectively. Alternatively, the parts can be doubled to emphasise the likeness. ROLFE goes on making notes. After a moment he looks up.)

ROLFE   *(turning on the charm)*   Ah, good-day, gentlemen. *(With a gracious nod to MRS. CROWE)* Thank you so much, Mrs. Crowe. *(He rises and moves R.)*

9

*(*MRS. CROWE *hovers in the hope of hearing something.)*

ROLFE   Please don't bother to wait. I shall see my visitors out myself.

*(*MRS. CROWE *exits reluctantly.* ROLFE *draws himself up to the full extent of his inconsiderable height to receive his guests. A trembling knee alone gives away his nervousness.)*

ROLFE   And now, gentlemen, please tell me how I can be of service to you.

FIRST BAILIFF *(looking at a document in his hand)*   Are you Mr. Corvo?

ROLFE *(suspiciously)*   No.

1ST BAILIFF *(looking at his papers)*   Sorry, sir. I mean *Baron* Corvo?

ROLFE   That is not my name.

2ND BAILIFF   We're try—

1ST BAILIFF *(consulting his papers)*   Oh. Then are you Frank W. Hochheimer?

(The SECOND BAILIFF *sits in the chair L.)*

ROLFE *(stiffly)*   No.

1ST BAILIFF   Or Mr. F. Austin?

ROLFE *(icily)* I am not.

2ND BAILIFF But you *are* Mr. Frederick William Rolfe *(he pronounces it as in "golf")*, are you not, sir?

ROLFE That is almost correct. My name is Frederick William *Rolfe*. *(He pronounces it as in "oaf.")* And who, may I ask, are you?

IST BAILIFF My colleague and I are Officers of the Court —Bailiffs, you understand—and we hold a writ against you, Mr. Rolfe *(handing the writ to* ROLFE*)* on behalf of certain parties—

*(*ROLFE *takes the writ and reads it.)*

IST BAILIFF —claiming certain debts. Do you follow me so far, Mr. Rolfe?

ROLFE Your brevity will assist my comprehension.

IST BAILIFF Quite so, sir. And I'm sure my colleague and I have no wish to remain here longer than necessary, so I will endeavour to constrict myself to the essential details, sir. The position is that, in brief, the Court has seen fit to award against you the initial sum of the debt plus the costs of the several plaintiffs versus Yourself for which a remittance must be made into Court forthwith in default of which and in consideration of a Warrant of Execution there will be no alternative but to attend at your premises and remove the contents thereof for sale by Public Auction.

ROLFE *(mumbling)* And then throw dice for my garments.

1ST BAILIFF   I beg your pardon?

2ND BAILIFF   'Scuse me asking, but are you by any chance a clergyman or anything of that sort? I mean—Fr. Rolfe —it looks a bit like Father Rolfe. See what I mean?

ROLFE   My name is Frederick Rolfe. I have never taken Holy Orders. Had I done so, no doubt I should have been a bishop by now—not a mere priest.

2ND BAILIFF   *(guffawing good-naturedly)*   Ho, ho, sir. Very good.

1ST BAILIFF   Well, I think if you're quite clear as to the nature of our call, sir, we . . .

ROLFE   You leave me in doubt as to the nature of your call.

1ST BAILIFF   *(producing a slip of paper)*   In that case perhaps you'd be good enough to sign this undertaking not to remove your furniture or effects or any part thereof from the premises until further notice.

ROLFE   You're asking me to sign this document?

1ST BAILIFF   That's right, sir. Just here.

ROLFE   I'm sorry, but that's something I never do.

1ST BAILIFF   What's that, sir?

ROLFE   Sign documents. I never sign documents.

1ST BAILIFF   Purely a formality, sir, I assure you.

ROLFE   You can assure me till the Day of Judgment, as many others have done before. Invariably their assurances were perfervid, perfidious, casuistic and, in a word, false. Ergo, no signature. Sorry.

1ST BAILIFF   Are you saying you are refusing to sign, sir?

ROLFE   I am saying in the simplest possible language that I do not intend to sign that document. Are you satisfied?

1ST BAILIFF   No, sir, I am not. If you refuse to sign this B sixty-three form here, I shall have no alternative but to apply immediately to the Court for a Warrant of Execution.

(The SECOND BAILIFF *rises and they both move up-stage.)*

1ST BAILIFF   You've not heard the last of this, I'm afraid, sir.

2ND BAILIFF   Good-day, sir.

(The BAILIFFS *exit.*
    Alone, ROLFE'S *flippant demeanour suddenly changes to that of savage rage. He tears off his collar and tie.)*

ROLFE *(through clenched teeth)*   Someone will have to suffer for this.

*(*MRS. CROWE *appears at the door.)*

MRS. CROWE   Are you by any chance speaking to me?

ROLFE *(quickly pulling himself together)* If I had heard your knock, Mrs. Crowe, I would have given myself the pleasure of addressing you, but since I did not . . . *(He sits in the armchair.)*

MRS. CROWE Perhaps you would be good enough to tell me who your callers were, Mr. Rolfe.

ROLFE I'm not aware that it is part of our contract that I have to identify my visitors.

MRS. CROWE You're in trouble again, aren't you? Were they the police?

ROLFE No.

MRS. CROWE *(moving downstage a pace)* Well, why wouldn't they give their names, then? Is it money? *(After a pause)* It is, isn't it?

ROLFE How can it be anything else? Of course it's money.

MRS. CROWE So they were bailiffs then?

> *(There is a silence while* MRS. CROWE *vacillates between her outraged feelings as a landlady and her concupiscent inclinations as a woman.)*

MRS. CROWE *(moving above his chair; in a wheedling voice)* Why don't you let me help you? I could help you—if you wanted me to. *(She leans over him.)* You know I have always wanted to be your friend. Couldn't I be now? Mr. Crowe left me quite comfortable. You know that. *(She puts her hand on his arm.)*

(In loathing at her touch ROLFE *jumps up, and in doing so kicks over the ink bottle on the floor in front of him. He hurries to wipe up the mess.)*

MRS. CROWE *(furious at the rejection of her advances)* There! *(Moving C)* Now look what you've done! Ink all over the floor! How do you suppose I'll ever get that out? It'll probably go right through the ceiling below.

ROLFE *(picking up the bottle)* I will naturally make good any damage done. *(He moves down R.)*

MRS. CROWE Make good any damage! With the bailiffs hardly out of the house? *(Working herself up)* I'm not fooled by your high-falutin' talk any more. Before you do any more of your "making good" you'll kindly pay me the quarter's rent you owe. Yes, and you'll kindly pay it by the end of the week as well or I shall be obliged to give you notice to leave. As a matter of fact, I need the room for a business gentleman.

ROLFE A business *gentleman?* Is there such a thing?

MRS. CROWE An old friend of yours.

ROLFE I haven't the slightest idea what you're talking about, neither have I any desire to . . . Who is this person?

MRS. CROWE Oh, I fancy you'll remember him all right. Don't you remember Belfast?

ROLFE Sant!

MRS. CROWE That's right, Mr. Rolfe. Mr. Jeremiah Sant.

ROLFE   Sant and that gutter scandal-sheet of his—what is it called? The *Tory Protester?*

MRS. CROWE   I want the room.

ROLFE   What excrement is he tooting out of his Orange flute now?

MRS. CROWE   It's none of your business. It's pay up or get out.

(She goes, deliberately not slamming the door.)

ROLFE *(shouting in a paroxysm of rage at the closed door)* You can't get shit from a wooden rocking-horse, you rapacious, concupiscent—female. *(After a short pause he has second thoughts, runs to the door, opens it, and shouts.)* Mrs. Crowe! Someone will have to suffer for this.

(There is no answer.)

ROLFE   Mrs. Crowe, I know you're listening. When you're sorry for what you've said, don't be afraid to say so, Mrs. Crowe. *(He closes the door and puts the blanket round his shoulders.)* Lascivious bitch. *(He rolls and lights a cigarette, holding it cupped in his two hands for warmth.)* All those curves and protuberances—breeding, that's all they're good for. *(He sits.)* Jeremiah Sant is a gerry-mandering gouger!

(After a moment he hears footsteps on the stairs again. He listens, wondering if it is MRS. CROWE *coming back to apologize. Instead, a letter is thrust under the door. He rises, looks at it suspiciously, then picks it up and turns it over, looking at the seal.)*

ROLFE   What—what's that? Archbishop's House? *(He tears the letter open and reads it with trembling hands. Savagely)* Hell and damnation! Imbeciles! Owl-like Hierarchs! Degenerates! *(After a pause)* God, if ever You loved me, hear me. They have denied me the priesthood again. Not a chance do You give me, God—ever. Listen! How can I serve You—*(to the crucifix)*—while You keep me so sequestered? I'm intelligent. So, O God, You made me. But intelligence must be active, potent, and perforce I am impotent and inactive always; futile in my loneliness. Why, O God, have You made me strange, uncommon, such a mystery to my fellow-creatures? Am I such a ruffian as to merit total exile from them? You have made me denuded of the power of love—to love anybody or be loved. I suppose I must go on like that to the end *(grimly)* because they are frightened of me—frightened of the labels I put on them. *(He puts out his cigarette savagely.)* Oh God, forgive me smoking. I quite forgot. I am not doing well at present, but what can I do? God, tell me clearly, unmistakably and distinctly, tell me, tell me what I must do—and make me do it. *(He sits.)* Oh Lord, I am sick—and very tired. *(His mind is in a ferment and he cannot rest.)*

(There is a knock on the door.)

ROLFE *(fiercely)*   Who is it?

(He rises and moves to L of the door.)

AGNES *(off)*   It's only me, sir.

ROLFE *(gently)*   Oh! All right. Come in, Agnes.

(AGNES, an elderly charlady, enters, wearing working

17

*clothes and an overall. She carries a tray on which is
a bowl of bread-and-milk and a newspaper.)*

AGNES I brought you a little bread-and-milk. Whatever
have you been saying to the Missus? Oh, well, never mind.
Here you are. Eat it up whilst it's hot.

ROLFE Thank you, Agnes. Please leave it.

(He turns away L.)

AGNES *(putting the tray on the chest)* My word, isn't it
chilly in here? Why ever haven't you turned on the . . .
*(She takes a quick look at ROLFE, sees that he is not paying
attention, fumbles for her purse, moves down R and, taking
out a coin, puts it in the meter.)*

ROLFE *(turning and seeing her)* Agnes, I forbid you . . .

AGNES *(taking matches from her apron and lighting the fire)*
Get along! Who d'you think you're forbidding then?

ROLFE *(moving over to warm himself)* You're a dear good
soul, Agnes, but you shouldn't have done that.

AGNES You can give it me back before I go to Mass Sunday.

ROLFE But Agnes . . .

AGNES I know you writing folk. I've had some in my time.

ROLFE I'm trying to tell you, Agnes, that I may not be able
to pay you back on Sunday.

AGNES Sunday? I'm sure I never said *next* Sunday. *(Moving*

18

to the door) Wait till the number comes up with your name on it and you can stand me a treat.

ROLFE *(moving to the chest)* So I will, Agnes, my word on it.

(He picks up the tray, takes it to his chair, sits, and starts to eat hungrily.)

AGNES I don't know why you don't go back to your painting. You had ever such a lovely touch with that.

(ROLFE is still guzzling up the bread-and-milk when his eyes fall on the newspaper. He picks it up and starts reading it, perfunctorily at first, then with ever-increasing interest.)

AGNES All those saints large as life. Some of them larger, I wouldn't be surprised.

(She begins to dust the mantelpiece, then the chest.)

ROLFE The Pope's dead.

AGNES *(not really listening)* Then there was your photography. I'm sure you could make a bit out of that—but you haven't got your camera now, have you?

ROLFE Agnes, the Pope is dead.

AGNES Yes, I know. God rest his soul. The poor old gentleman.

ROLFE *(reading from the paper)* "A Conclave of the Sacred College is to be convened immediately in order to elect a successor to the Holy See."

AGNES Perhaps they'll choose our own Archbishop this time.

ROLFE *(continuing to read)* "In accordance with the Council of Lateran, the votes of two-thirds of the Cardinals present at the Conclave will be required for the election of the Supreme Pontiff. A Vatican expert reports, however, that with the present alignment among the various factions in the Sacred College, it is by no means easy to see how a clear two-thirds majority can be achieved. He goes on to suggest . . ."

AGNES It's about time they had an English Pope for a change.

(ROLFE turns to stare at her.)

AGNES There—I've finished you now, Mr. Rolfe. See you tomorrow, then.

(AGNES exits.
ROLFE stares after her for a brief moment. Then he rises, replaces the tray on the chest, takes a fat-looking reference book from the mantelpiece and looks something up in the index. He sits, takes up his paper and pencil and starts to write rapidly with occasional reference to the book.)

ROLFE English Pope. Seven-seventy-two to seven-ninety-five, Hadrian the First. Eight-sixty-nine to eight-seventy-two, Hadrian the Second. Eight-eighty-four to eight-eighty-five—not very long, that one—Hadrian the Third. Ah—here we are. Eleven-fifty-four to eleven-fifty-nine, Nicholas Breakspeare, Hadrian the Fourth. Ha! Son of a monk!

(There is a pause while he flips through the reference book again.) Hadrian the Fifth, a Genoese. Hadrian the Sixth, that's right, from Utrecht. *(He continues to write, with great energy, for a moment or two.)* Hadrian the Fourth . . . Hadrian the Fifth . . . Hadrian the Sixth . . . Hadrian the Seventh. In mind he was tired, worn out by years of hope deferred, of loneliness, of unrewarded toil.

> *(There is a change in the lighting to a warmer hue. After a few moments,* ROLFE *is interrupted by a knock at the door.)*

ROLFE   Who is it?

> *(*MRS. CROWE *opens the door.)*

MRS. CROWE   There are two gentlemen downstairs to see you.

ROLFE   Not now.

MRS. CROWE   They're clergymen.

ROLFE   Clergymen. Come in, Mrs. Crowe.

> *(*MRS. CROWE *enters the room.)*

ROLFE   What sort of clergymen?

MRS. CROWE   I couldn't really say. One's an elderly gentleman, all in red and black. The other is much younger with bits of purple.

ROLFE   His Grace the Archbishop of Pimlico, and the Bishop of Caerleon—of course.

MRS. CROWE *(more intrigued than ever)*   Oh. You were expecting them then?

ROLFE   They are not entirely unexpected. Now perhaps you would be good enough to . . .

MRS. CROWE   Yes, I'll bring them up.

> *(*MRS. CROWE *exits.*
>
> ROLFE *rushes to pick up his tie and collar and puts them on in front of the mirror. This done, he quickly adopts a dignified posture to receive his visitors.*
>
> *After a pause* MRS. CROWE *shows in* DR. COURTLEIGH *and* DR. TALACRYN.)*

MRS. CROWE   This way, gentlemen. I'm sorry for all the stairs. Oh dear, I'm quite out of breath myself.

ROLFE   Come in. *Thank* you, Mrs. Crowe.

MRS. CROWE   I just wondered if your guests would like some tea . . .

ROLFE   Not for the moment, thank you.

MRS. CROWE   Very well.

> *(*MRS. CROWE *exits.*
>
> COURTLEIGH *moves down* C, TALACRYN *down LC.)*

TALACRYN   Your Eminence, may I present Mr. Rolfe . . .

(ROLFE ignores COURTLEIGH, *goes straight to* TALA-
CRYN, *kneels to him and kisses the episcopal ring on
his hand. He then returns R.)*

ROLFE *(to* COURTLEIGH*)* Your Eminence will understand
that I do not wish to be disrespectful, but the Bishop of
Caerleon calls himself my friend.

COURTLEIGH I hope, Mr. Rolfe, that you will accept my
blessing as well as Dr. Talacryn's.

(ROLFE kneels and kisses the cardinalatial ring.)

ROLFE Please sit down—as best you may.

(COURTLEIGH sits C. TALACRYN stands L of him.)

TALACRYN Freddy, His Eminence wishes to ask you a few
questions and he thought you would not take it amiss if
I were present—as your friend.

*(ROLFE acknowledges TALACRYN's remark and turns
to COURTLEIGH.)*

COURTLEIGH Mr. Rolfe, it has recently been brought to
my remembrance that you were at one time a candidate
for Holy Orders. I am aware of all the—ah—unpleasantness which attended that portion of your career; but it
is only lately that I have fully realized that you yourself
have never accepted or acquiesced in the verdict of your
superiors.

ROLFE I never have accepted it. I have never acquiesced in
it. I never will accept it. I never will acquiesce in it.

COURTLEIGH   Quite, er . . .

ROLFE   But I nourish no grudge and seek no revenge. I am content to lead my own life, avoiding all my brother Catholics when circumstances throw them—

(COURTLEIGH *gets restive.*)

ROLFE   —in my path. I don't squash cockroaches.

COURTLEIGH   And the effect upon your soul?

ROLFE   The effect upon my soul is perfectly ghastly. I have lost faith in man, and I have lost the power of loving. I have become a rudderless derelict.

COURTLEIGH   How terrible!

ROLFE   Terrible? Yes, it is indeed terrible. And, as head of the Roman Communion in this country, let the blame be upon you for the destruction of this soul.

(COURTLEIGH *raises his hands in protest.*)

ROLFE   As for your myrmidons, I spit upon them and defy them and you may rest assured that I shall continue to fight them as long as I can hold a pen.

COURTLEIGH   Would you mind telling me your reasons?

ROLFE   I should have to say very disagreeable things, Eminence.

COURTLEIGH   Tell me the truth.

ROLFE   The Catholic and Apostolic Church, with its championing of learning and beauty, was always to me a real and living thing. It was with the highest hopes, therefore, that I entered Oscott College to begin my career as a Clerk in Holy Orders. I was soon obliged to leave, however, after a dispute with the Principal, who seemed to see no offence in grubs grazing on the lettuces and caterpillars cantering across the refectory table. The Archbishop of Agneda then invited me, on recommendation, to attend St. Andrew's College at Rome. I gladly went, on the assurance that my expenses would be borne by the Archbishop. They never were and, in consequence, I was several hundred pounds out of pocket.

COURTLEIGH   Dear me!

> (*He looks at* TALACRYN *for confirmation.*
> TALACRYN *nods agreement.*)

COURTLEIGH   Yes?

ROLFE   Then after four months in college, I was expelled suddenly and brutally.

COURTLEIGH   And what reason was given?

ROLFE   No reason was ever given. The gossip of my fellow-students—immature cubs prone to acne and versed in dog Latin—was that I had no Vocation.

COURTLEIGH   I see. Go on.

ROLFE   Then there was the occasion in Wales when the machinations of a certain cleric, whose cloven hoof defiled the shrine of the Blessed Saint Winifred of Holywell, defrauded me of my rightful desserts for two years of arduous work undertaken at his request. Having been robbed by the said priest not only of my means of livelihood, but also of health, comfort, friends and reputation, and brought physically to my knees, he then gave me the *coup de grace* by debarring me from the Sacraments. I then had no option but to leave Wales and start life from scratch. *(Crossing below the others to L)* I walked to London. Two hundred and fourteen miles. It took me eighteen days.

COURTLEIGH Good gracious! But did no one come forward to assist you at this time?

ROLFE No one except the Bishop of Caerleon, who somewhat belatedly received me back into Communion. Eventually, others, moved no doubt by the last twitchings of their dying consciences, made tentative overtures. To these I quoted St. Matthew twenty-five, verses forty-one to forty-three.

COURTLEIGH Now, how does that go?

(He feels in the air with his hand for the quotation.)

ROLFE From "I was hungered and ye gave me no meat" down to "Depart from me ye cursed, into aeonial fire."

COURTLEIGH You are hard, Mr. Rolfe, very hard.

ROLFE I am what you and your fellow Catholics have made me.

COURTLEIGH Poor child—poor child.

ROLFE I request Your Eminence will not speak to me in

that tone. I disdain your pity at this date. The catastrophe is complete.

COURTLEIGH My son, have you never caught yourself thinking kindly of your former friends? You cannot always be in a state of white-hot rage, you know.

ROLFE Yes, Eminence, there are some with whom, strange to say, I would wish to be reconciled—when my anger is not dynamic, that is. *(He smiles.)* But they do not come to me—as you have come.

COURTLEIGH They probably do not wish to expose themselves to—ah—quotations from St. Matthew's gospel.

ROLFE Did I heave china-ware at Your Lordship?

TALACRYN You did not. *(To* COURTLEIGH*)* Your Eminence, I believe I understand Mr. Rolfe's frame of mind. A burned child dreads the fire.

COURTLEIGH True. And what course did you embark on then, Mr. Rolfe?

ROLFE I determined to occupy my energies with some pursuit for which my nature fitted me, until the Divine Giver of my Vocation should deign to manifest it to others as well as myself. I took to painting and writing. I began to write simply because, by this time, I had an imperious necessity to say certain things. *(He sits in the chair L.)* In any case, ultimate penury denied me access to painting materials. So literature is now the only outlet you Catholics have left me—and believe me, I have very much to say.

COURTLEIGH You have not perhaps many kindly feelings towards me personally, Mr. Rolfe.

ROLFE I have no kindly feelings at all towards Your Eminence, but I trust I shall never be found wanting in reverence towards your sacred purple. I am only speaking civilly to you because you are a successor to Augustine and Theodore Dunstan and Anselm, Chichele and Chichester, and because for the nonce, my friend the Bishop of Caerleon has made you my guest.

COURTLEIGH Well, well!

ROLFE My Lord Cardinal, I do not know what you want of me, nor why you have come.

COURTLEIGH I wished first of all to know if you still remained Catholic.

ROLFE If I still remained Catholic!

COURTLEIGH People who have been denied the priesthood have been known to commit apostasy.

ROLFE Rest assured, Eminence, I am not in revolt against the Faith, but against the Faithful.

COURTLEIGH *(trying not to get angry)* I am trying to determine whether or not, at the time of which we are speaking, you formed any opinion of your own concerning your Vocation, Mr. Rolfe.

ROLFE No.

COURTLEIGH No?

ROLFE No. My opinion concerning my Vocation for the priesthood had been formed when I was a boy of fifteen. I have never relinquished my Divine Gift.

COURTLEIGH You persist?

ROLFE Your Eminence, I am not a bog-trotting Fenian or one of your Sauchiehall Street hybrids—but English and sure; born under Cancer. Naturally I persist.

COURTLEIGH But the man to whom Divine Providence vouchsafes a Vocation is bound to pursue it. *You* are practising as an author.

ROLFE This is only a means to an end. *(Rising)* When I shall have earned enough to pay my debts, I shall go straight to Rome and fix the profligate priest who sacked me.

COURTLEIGH *(throwing up his hands)* Ssh!

TALACRYN *(quickly)* Your Eminence mustn't be offended by Mr. Rolfe's satirical turn of phrase. He is not the man to smite those who have done him ill.

ROLFE Do not deceive yourself, My Lord. So long as we recruit our spiritual pastors from the hooligan class, I shall smite them with all my strength.

COURTLEIGH Really, Mr. Rolfe!

TALACRYN You're a little beside the point, Freddy.

ROLFE Under the circumstances, His Eminence will indulge me. I've had enough of being buffeted by bishops.

Until I'm the possessor of a cheque book I do not propose to start commerce with the clergy again.

(There is a pause while COURTLEIGH *looks into space and* TALACRYN *looks at his toes.)*

COURTLEIGH Frederick William Rolfe, I summon you to offer yourself to me.

ROLFE *(after a pause: quietly)* I am not ready to offer myself to Your Eminence.

COURTLEIGH Not ready?

ROLFE I hoped I had made it clear that, in regard to my Vocation, I am marking time until I shall have earned enough to pay my debts which were so monstrously incurred on me.

COURTLEIGH You keep harping on that string.

ROLFE It is the only string you have left unbroken on my lute.

COURTLEIGH Well, well; the money question need not trouble you.

ROLFE But it does trouble me. And your amazing summons troubles me as well. Why do you come to me after all these years?

COURTLEIGH It is precisely because of these years—how many was it?

ROLFE Call it twenty.

COURTLEIGH —that we must take your singular persistency as proof of the genuineness of your Vocation. And therefore, I am here today to summon you to accept Holy Orders with no delay beyond the canonical intervals.

ROLFE In two years' time, when I shall have published three more books, I will respond to your summons. Not till then.

TALACRYN But His Eminence has said that the money question need not hinder you.

ROLFE Yes, and the Archbishop of Agneda said the same.

(COURTLEIGH *looks as if he is going to explode, and* TALACRYN *hastens to intervene.*)

TALACRYN I am witness of His Eminence's words, Freddy.

ROLFE What's the good of that? Supposing in a couple of months His Eminence chooses to alter his mind? Could I hail a prince of the church before a secular tribunal? Would I? Could I subpoena Your Lordship to testify against your Metropolitan and Provincial? (*Crossing below to down R*) Could I? Would I? Would you?

(COURTLEIGH *makes as if to interject, but* ROLFE *cuts in.*)

ROLFE My Lord Cardinal, I must speak, and you must hear me. You are offering me the Priesthood on good and legitimate grounds, for which I thank God. But, if I correctly interpret you, you are also offering me something in the shape of money, and I will be no man's pensioner.

COURTLEIGH *(mildly)* Please understand me, Mr. Rolfe, that the monies in question are being offered solely as restitution for the years in which you were denied the Priesthood.

ROLFE Oh! *(After a pause)* No, I will not take charity.

TALACRYN Well, then, Freddy, in what form will you accept this act of justice from us? Do make an effort to believe we are sincerely in earnest and that in this matter we are in your hands. *(Turning to* COURTLEIGH*)* I may say that, Your Eminence?

COURTLEIGH Unreservedly.

(There is a pause while ROLFE *considers.)*

ROLFE *(quietly but with determination)* I will accept a written expression of regret for the wrongs which have been done to me by both Your Eminence and by others who have followed your advice, command or example.

COURTLEIGH *(taking a folded piece of paper from his breviary)* It is here.

ROLFE *(at first surprised, then reading it with care)* I thank Your Eminence. *(He tears the paper into pieces.)* —and all my brother Catholics.

COURTLEIGH Man alive!

ROLFE I do not care to preserve a record of my superiors' humiliation.

COURTLEIGH *(with an effort)*   I see that Mr. Rolfe knows how to behave nobly, Frank.

ROLFE   Only now and again. But I had long ago arranged to do just that.

> *(The prelates make a gesture of incomprehension to each other.* COURTLEIGH *stands.* ROLFE *kneels and receives benedictions.)*

COURTLEIGH   We shall see you then at Archbishop's House tomorrow morning, Mr. Rolfe.

ROLFE   I will be there at half-past seven to confess to the Bishop of Caerleon. Your Eminence says Mass at eight and will give me to Holy Communion. Then, if it please Your Eminence, you will give me the four Minor Orders. In the meantime, I will go and have a Turkish bath and buy myself a Roman collar.

> *(*COURTLEIGH *moves to the door.*
> ROLFE *goes quickly up and opens it.* COURTLEIGH *exits.*
> TALACRYN *is about to follow.)*

ROLFE   Your Lordship doesn't happen to know the price of collars these days?

TALACRYN *(apologetically)*   I haven't the slightest idea, I'm afraid.

ROLFE   Well then, just to be on the safe side, perhaps you wouldn't mind springing me a fiver.

TALACRYN *(embarrassed)*   Oh, certainly. Certainly. *(He*

fumbles in his pockets for his wallet. Eventually he finds it and gives a banknote to ROLFE.*)* Thank you.

ROLFE *(graciously)* Not at all. See you tomorrow.

> (TALACRYN *exits, leaving the door open.*
> ROLFE *goes to the mirror, takes off his tie and turns his collar back to front. He then gives his reflection an episcopal blessing. Suddenly he freezes. He sees a reflection of somebody behind him. He turns round to see* JEREMIAH SANT *standing in the doorway.)*

ROLFE Sant!

SANT Still at your play-acting, I see! What part is it this time?

ROLFE What are you doing in here?

SANT I've come to look at my room.

ROLFE *Your* room?

SANT Aye. I've been given to understand that you've got your marching orders again.

ROLFE What do you mean?

SANT *(moving down C)* The Order of the Boot. You're out. Just like old times, isn't it?

ROLFE *(changing tactics)* Yes, as a matter of fact I do have to leave here as it happens. I've been summoned for work elsewhere.

SANT   Summoned, have ye? Summonsed, more likely, from what I know of you.

ROLFE *(crossing L)*   Meanwhile this room is mine until the end of the week.

SANT   Aye, if you've paid the rent.

ROLFE   Get out of here.

SANT   Oh, aye, I'm going, but I'll be back on Saturday, so make sure you're away by then.

ROLFE   What makes you persist in hounding me?

SANT   You really want an answer? Read Revelations seventeen. Do you know how it goes?

ROLFE   I do not.

SANT   Like this: "And there came one of the seven angels, saying unto me, come hither; I will shew unto thee the judgement of the great whore that sitteth upon many waters: With whom the kings of the earth have committed fornication, and the inhabitants of the earth have been made drunk with the wine of her fornication—"

ROLFE   Orange Day rantings!

SANT   Let me finish—"So he carried me away in the spirit into the wilderness: and I saw a woman sit upon a scarlet coloured beast, full of names of blasphemy, having seven heads and ten horns . . ." As far as I'm concerned you're all seven of those heads and all ten of the horns—because you worked for me once. Remember?

ROLFE It is not a memory I cherish.

SANT Likely not. A fake, a liar and a cheat hardly likes to be shown up for what is really is.

ROLFE You've no cause to say that.

SANT Haven't I? Haven't I? You think I don't know what went on in Skene Street? You think I don't know why they carried you out into the street, in your bed for all to see?

> (ROLFE *winces at this recollection which obviously hits below the belt.*)

SANT Aye! That got ye, didn't it? "And the beast was taken, and with him the false prophet that received the mask of the beast. These were both cast alive into a lake of fire burning with brimstone!"

ROLFE Ravings of a bog-trotting lunatic.

SANT Lunatic, is it? Who's the biggest lunatic, you or me? When your lot go to Communion and eat that wafer, you believe it's the body, blood and bones of Jesus Christ, don't ye? That makes you a Cannibal, doesn't it?

ROLFE Not on a Friday.

SANT Ugh, you make me puke, you dirty Popehead.

ROLFE Get out.

SANT All right friend, you asked a question and I've given you the answer. (*He makes for the door.*) As the Lord saith, an eye for an eye and a tooth for a tooth. I'm not finished with you yet. *(He stops with his hand on the door-handle.)* When you go leave the window wide, will ye. It's the smell of a Papish I can't abide. *(Shouting)* God save Britain from Popery! No surrender!

(SANT *exits, leaving the door open, and singing as he goes, "The Sash My Father Wore."*)

SANT   "Our Father knew the Rome of old
And evil is thy fame.
Thy kind embrace the galling chain,
Thy kiss the blazing flame."

(ROLFE *rises and stands quite still for a moment. His triumphant mood has vanished and, once more, he looks trapped and hunted. After a moment's thought he springs into action. Pulling a holdall out from the corner up C he puts it on the chair, takes a few effects from the chest-of-drawers and throws them in, then goes to the door and listens to make sure the coast is clear. Having satisfied himself on this count he picks up the holdall and tiptoes out, as the lights fade to a*

BLACKOUT.)

SCENE TWO

A room in Archbishop's House. Seven-thirty the following morning.

 The only furniture is an upright armchair set C and facing at an angle up LC, and a thick cushion set close L of the chair.

 As the lights come up, TALACRYN *enters from an opening up R and moves to the chair. A moment later* ROLFE *enters up L.*

TALACRYN Good morning, Freddy. I hope your new lodgings are comfortable.

ROLFE Compared to Broadhurst Gardens, they are as the Elysian Fields.

TALACRYN I never cared much for N.W.6 either. *(He sits in the chair, facing up LC.)* Now—shall we get this over?

ROLFE It may take rather a long time.

TALACRYN All day if necessary.

 (He takes a small violet stole which he has been carry-

*ing on his arm, kisses the cross embroidered on it, and
puts it round his shoulders. He then sits in the chair,
facing up LC.*

*ROLFE kneels on the cushion facing downstage, so
that he has a three-quarter back view of the BISHOP.
He makes the sign of the cross.*

*Both skip through the ritual beginning and end
of the confession pretty fast.)*

ROLFE   Bless me, Father, for I have sinned.

TALACRYN   May the Lord be in thine heart and on thy lips,
that thou with truth and humility mayest confess thy sins
(He makes the sign of the cross), in the name of the Father
and of the Son and of the Holy Ghost, Amen.

ROLFE   I last confessed five days ago.

TALACRYN   Since then, my son?

ROLFE   Since then I broke the first commandment by being
superstitiously silly enough to come downstairs in my socks
because I had accidentally put on my left shoe before my
right. I broke the third commandment by permitting my
mind to be distracted by the palpably Dublin accent of the
Priest who said Mass on Saturday.

TALACRYN   Is there nothing more on your conscience, my
son?

ROLFE   Lots. I confess that I have broken the sixth commandment by continuing to read an epigram in the An-

thology after I had found out that it was obscene. I have
broken the third commandment of the Church by eating
dripping toast for tea on Friday. I was hungry; it was very
nice. I made a good meal of it and couldn't eat any dinner.
This was thoughtless at first, then wilful.

TALACRYN Are you bound to fast this Lent?

ROLFE Yes, Father. I should now like to make a general
confession of the chief sins of my life.

TALACRYN Proceed, my son.

ROLFE I earnestly desire to do God's will in all things, but
I often fail. I like to worship my Maker alone, unseen of all
save him. That is why I cannot hear Mass with devotion
in those churches where one is obliged to squat in a pew
like a Protestant, with other people's hot and filthy breath
blowing down my neck. My mind has a twist towards fri-
volity, towards perversity. I have been irreverent and dis-
obedient to my superiors. For example, I said that the
legs of a certain domestic prelate were formed like little
Jacobean communion-rails.

(TALACRYN *reacts slightly to this last.*)

ROLFE I have told improper stories—not of the revolting
kind, but those which are witty, anti-Protestant—the sort
common among the clergy. Being anti-pathetic to fish, I
once made an enemy sick by the filthy comparison which I
used in regard to some oysters which he was about to eat.
I confess that two or three times in my life I have delighted in impure thoughts inspired by some lines in
Cicero's *Oration for Marcus Coelius.*

TALACRYN   I don't for the moment recall—well, never mind. Is there nothing further?

ROLFE   There is one thing which I have never mentioned in confession except in vague terms only.

TALACRYN   Relieve your mind, my son.

ROLFE   Father, I confess I have not kept my senses in proper custody. Sometimes I catch myself extracting elements of aesthetic enjoyment from unaesthetic situations.

TALACRYN   Can you be more precise, my son?

ROLFE   Yes, well, for example, I once was present at the amputation of a leg. Under anaesthetics, directly the saw touched the marrow of the thigh bone, the other leg began to kick. I was next to it, and the surgeon told me to hold it still. It was ghastly, but I did. And then I actually caught myself admiring the exquisite silky texture of the human skin. Father, I am a very sorry Christian. I confess all these sins, all the sins which I cannot remember, all the sins of my life. I implore pardon of God; and from thee, O Father, penance and absolution. *(Quickly)* Therefore, I beseech blessed Mary Ever-Virgin.

TALACRYN   My son, do you love God?

(From silence, tardily the response emerges.)

ROLFE   I don't know. I really don't know. He is the Maker of the World to me. He is Truth and Righteousness and Beauty. He is first. He is last. He is Lord of all to me. I absolutely believe in Him. I unconditionally trust Him.

I am ready and willing to make any kind of sacrifice for Him. So far I clearly see. Then in my mind, there comes a great gap—filled with fog.

TALACRYN   Do you love your neighbour?

ROLFE   Hmm?

TALACRYN   Do you love your neighbour?

ROLFE   Oh. No. Frankly, I detest him—and her. Most people are repulsive to me, because they are ugly in person, or in manner, or in mind. I have met those with whom I should like to be in sympathy, but I have been unable to get near enough to them.

TALACRYN   Could you not love them?

ROLFE   No.

TALACRYN   Do you love yourself?

ROLFE   On the whole, I think I despise myself, body, mind and soul. I do look after my body and cultivate my mind. And naturally I stick up for myself, but—no, my body and mind are no particular pleasure to me.

TALACRYN   Have you nothing else to confess, my son?

ROLFE   Nothing. Really nothing, Father. I am very tired. I long to be at rest.

TALACRYN   That is actually the longing of your soul for God. Cultivate that longing, my son, for it will lead you to love

Him. Thank Him with all your heart for this great gift of longing. At the same time remember the words of Christ our Saviour: "If ye Love Me, keep My Commandments." Remember, He definitely commands you to love your neighbour. Serve the servants of God, and you will learn to love God. You have tasted the pleasures of this world and they are as ashes in your mouth. In the tremendous dignity to which you have been called—the dignity of the priesthood—you will be subject to fiercer temptations than those which have assaulted you in the past. Brace the great natural strength of your will to resist them. Begin to love your neighbour so that you may soon consciously come to love God. My son, the key to all your difficulties, past, present and to come, is love. For your penance, you will say—no, the penance for Minor Orders is rather long—for your penance you will say the Divine Praises with the celebrant after Mass. And now—

(The ritual is gabbled through, ROLFE *repeating quickly after* TALACRYN.)*

TALACRYN   O my God, most worthy of all love—I grieve from my heart for having sinned against Thee—And I purpose by Thy Grace—Never more to offend Thee for the time to come.

*(*TALACRYN *continues alone, making the sign of the cross.)*

TALACRYN   Ego te absolvo in Nomine Patris et Filii et Spiritus Sancti, Amen. Go in peace and pray for me.

*(*ROLFE *and* TALACRYN *rise and move downstage together.* TALACRYN *resumes his informal manner.)*

43

TALACRYN   But before you do, I have been instructed by His Eminence to inform you that you will accompany him to Rome tomorrow.

ROLFE   To Rome!

TALACRYN   You will act as his private chaplain at the Conclave which is to elect the new Pope. We will travel together, Freddy.

> (ROLFE *and* TALACRYN *move upstage towards the exit R.*
> *A single bell starts to toll insistently. An echoing liturgy is distantly heard as the lights fade to a*
>
> BLACKOUT.)

SCENE THREE

A chapel in the Vatican.

As the lights come up, a bell tolls in the distance and the liturgy continues to be heard in some remote side chapel. The only furnishings are two candelabra, up RC and LC. Two ACOLYTES *(boys) in surplices enter, from up R and up L, genuflect in unison towards the direction of the altar, and proceed to light the candelabra with long tapers. Having done so, they genuflect again, and both exit up R.*

TALACRYN and ROLFE *enter together up L. Their hands are folded, clasping breviaries.* ROLFE, *now in Holy Orders, wears a black soutane and biretta.* TALACRYN *wears similar garb suitable to a bishop.*

As they speak the following dialogue, they perambulate round the stage together.

ROLFE *(sniffing at the smell of incense)* Nothing stinks like the odour of sanctity.

TALACRYN Now, now.

ROLFE *(pointing out front)* Look at those frescos. Wasn't it Mark Twain who said: "The Creator made Italy from designs by Michelangelo"?

TALACRYN *(distrait)* Very possibly. Their Eminences are still sitting, it seems.

ROLFE   On two addled eggs apiece.

TALACRYN   Freddy, I beg you—the whole world is waiting for the imminent announcement of a new Pope, and you make jokes in rather doubtful taste.

ROLFE   Let me assure Your Lordship that my flippancy in no way reflects my concern with the outcome of the Sacred Consistory. I've studied the form of those members of the Sacred College who could be said to be possible starters for the Supreme Pontificate, and it's my belief that the short-odds favourite . . .

TALACRYN   Short-odds favourite!

ROLFE   A sporting metaphor, indicating . . .

TALACRYN   I am acquainted with the jargon of the Turf, Freddy.

ROLFE   Then if I may continue the analogy, it's perfectly plain to a student of form that the short-odds favourite must be the present Secretary of State, Cardinal Ragna, whom God preserve.

TALACRYN   Not everyone would say "Amen" to that, I fear.

ROLFE   But then there is the malpractice called "Bumping and Boring"—

TALACRYN   —much frowned upon by the stewards—

ROLFE —and I very much doubt whether Cardinal Ragna will be allowed to trot away with the race. Our own Archbishop, for example, would nominate the Parish Priest of Ballyjamesduff if it would keep Ragna out.

TALACRYN Steady.

ROLFE And I'm prepared to bet a thousand pound to a penny-halfpenny stamp that the Conclave has broken down again for the simple reason that Ragna's been nobbled.

TALACRYN *(smiling)* I wish I had it in me to be quite so irreverent as you, Freddy.

ROLFE Perhaps, but I doubt if Your Lordship has it in him to be quite so devout either. You are a natural Christian, My Lord Bishop. I, on the other hand, am a religious maniac.

TALACRYN You do yourself an injustice.

ROLFE *(casually)* I know I do. *(Looking up at a fresco on the ceiling)* Isn't that superb? *(Pointing)* Look at that. A little lacking in generosity in describing—*(he makes a graphic gesture)*—but compared to a figure like that, what can people see to admire in the female form?

TALACRYN It's a matter of taste, I suppose.

ROLFE *(looking at* TALACRYN*)* What a waste!

TALACRYN What is a waste?

ROLFE That such a fine, upstanding man as Your Lordship

47

should have felt inclined to accept the celibacy of priest-hood.

TALACRYN   Good heavens, Freddy. If you are being serious, I can assure you that from the moment I took Orders no other thought ever occurred to me.

ROLFE   Nevertheless one has to admit that the vestigial nipples on a man are about as useful as the Pontifical pudenda. Had I been a Renaissance Pope, I should have in-sisted that ...

(A bell begins to clang insistently.)

ROLFE   Something seems to be happening.

*(*ROLFE *moves down* L. TALACRYN *follows to* R *of him.)*

TALACRYN   I think they must have risen.

ROLFE   Who?

TALACRYN   The Cardinals-Compromissory.

ROLFE   Will they have reached a decision?

TALACRYN   We shall soon see. Here they come.

(The nine CARDINALS-COMPROMISSORY, *in full purple, led by the* BEARERS, *appear from the rear of the audi-torium and move in procession down the aisles to the stage, chanting the* Christus Vincit *as they move.*
   Arriving on the stage, they form an arc from R to above TALACRYN *LC. The* CARDINAL-ARCHDEACON

remains extreme R. Lastly comes an ACOLYTE *bearing
the Papal crown—the triple tiara—on a cushion. All
bow in the direction of the altar, then turn inwards.
As soon as everyone is in position the bell ceases.)*

ROLFE *(in a whisper to* TALACRYN*)* What is it? What is
happening?

TALACRYN   I think God has given us a Pope.

ROLFE   Whom?

(The litany ceases, and all turn to face ROLFE *and*
TALACRYN. *All except* ROLFE *kneel.)*

CARDINAL-ARCHDEACON   Reverend Lord, the Sacred College
has elected Thee to be the successor to St. Peter. Wilt thou
accept pontificality?

(Since all present are now facing towards ROLFE *and*
TALACRYN, ROLFE *assumes it is the latter who is being
addressed. He turns towards* TALACRYN *with a happy
smile.* TALACRYN, *however, is kneeling. Confused,*
ROLFE *turns back to look at the* CARDINAL-ARCH-
DEACON.*)*

CARDINAL-ARCHDEACON *(with greater emphasis)*   Reverend
Lord, the Sacred College has elected Thee to be the successor to St. Peter. Wilt thou accept pontificality?

(There is another pause. ROLFE, *looking round to
where all are on their knees facing inwards towards
him, at last realizes that the awful question is addressed to him.)*

ROLFE Will *I?*

TALACRYN *(in a whisper)* The response is *Volo*—or *Nolo.*

(ROLFE *takes a deep breath, crossing his right hand over his left on his breast.)*

ROLFE *Volo*—I will.

(As organ peals out, as—

THE CURTAIN FALLS.*)*

ACT TWO

SCENE ONE

When the curtain rises, MRS. CROWE *is seated upstage on the chaise-longue, with* JEREMIAH SANT *beside her. Both have drinks in their hands.*

SANT *is a member of the F.R.S.—Fellowship of Religious Segregation, an extremist group, outlawed in Ulster, dedicated to the persecution of Roman Catholics in general and the Pope in particular. He also runs a rabble-rousing newspaper called* The Tory Protestor *dedicated to the same aims.* SANT *himself is a violent and dangerous fanatic.*

MRS. CROWE *is reading aloud from a newspaper.*

MRS. CROWE   Where are we? Yes, here it is— ". . . and as representatives of the Catholic world looked on, the Triple Crown was placed on the head of Frederick William Rolfe, the first English Pope to ascend the Throne of St. Peter since eleven-fifty-four when Nicholas Brakespeare became Pope Hadrian the Fourth . . ."

SANT   Holy God, doesn't it make you want to puke! To think of an Englishman sinking so low. What paper is that, anyway?

MRS. CROWE   The *Daily Mirror.*

SANT Well just listen to what the old *Protestor* has got to say. You'll have no trouble identifying the writer. *(He takes a copy of his own newspaper out of his pocket and starts to read.)* "Recent sorry events in Rome must remind all True Blue Ulstermen that we will never bow down to those who are trying to sell us lock, stock and barrel to Popery. We will have no truck with the English traitor who calls himself the Pope. He may call himself Pope, but we call him the Roman anti-christ. Let us be reminded of Papist policy in Ulster. They intend to *breed* us out. But the wall of separation reaches to Highest Heaven. We will not allow the rights of the individual, nor the rights of the family, to be interfered with by a debauched priesthood. We had said 'No Surrender' before and we say 'No Surrender' again now. And we shall continue to say 'Keep the Union Jack flying for God and Ulster' " . . . That's telling 'em, hey Nancy?

MRS. CROWE Oh, that's very good Jerry . . . but—

SANT —but what?

MRS. CROWE I can never understand what there is to get so excited about.

SANT Get so excited! *(Rising and moving L)* Rome rule means Home Rule, doesn't it? But I'm thinking maybe the Papishes have cooked their own goose this time.

MRS. CROWE How's that then?

SANT Well, for one thing, this will queer the pitch for the Home Rulers. One false move and it could be civil war in

Ireland with the Fenians cutting each other's dirty throats. And a good job too. They'll not stand for an Englishman giving out the orders, Pope or no.

MRS. CROWE   Oh, I'll never understand Irish politics as long as I live. Here, let me fill your glass.

SANT   Aye, you do that, sweetheart.

(There is a pause. SANT has now blown off most of his steam. MRS. CROWE fills both glasses.)

MRS. CROWE   Looking after men—that's something I do understand.

SANT   True for you, Nancy. *(He sits beside her.)* Never a truer word. *(He raises his glass.)* Good luck!

MRS. CROWE   Here's cheers.

SANT   But there's one thing I've never been able to find out—what you see in that abomination of desolation.

MRS. CROWE   Who?

SANT   Rolfe.

MRS. CROWE   What *I* see in *him?* Oh, please, Jerry. Give me a little credit. Do you know what he used to do? No, I don't want to talk about it. I can't bear to speak about him any more.

(She starts to snivel.)

SANT   Now just a moment, Nancy. Just a moment. *(He rises and moves below the chaise-longue to R of the table and picks up the bottle.)* Here, give us your glass.

MRS. CROWE *(upset)*   Oh, no thank you, Jerry.

SANT   Come on, sweetheart. Just a half 'un.

MRS. CROWE   Oh, all right then.

> *(SANT fills both glasses and sits again. They drink. MRS. CROWE makes a face.)*

MRS. CROWE   Oooh, this is strong.

> *(She downs it in one nevertheless.)*

SANT   Never mind. It'll do you good. Now, Nance, just now you started to say something, and by-and-by you're going to finish it. But first I'm going to tell you one or two things.

MRS. CROWE   What things?

SANT   Well, first, how would you like to come on a wee trip with me to Rome?

MRS. CROWE   To Rome? But, Jerry, how could I? I mean . . .

SANT   Oh, don't you worry about that. We'll be properly chaperoned, I promise you.

MRS. CROWE   But I've got nothing to wear.

SANT   No problem at all. As you know, I am an F.R.S.

MRS. CROWE   A what?

SANT   A Senior Brother of the Fellowship of Religious Segregation, who are very disturbed by certain recent events and, as loyal servants of the Crown, we feel it our duty to do whatever we can to protect the Free Churches of the United Kingdom.

(*He gets up and postures round the room.*)

MRS. CROWE   Yes, Jerry, but what's all this to do with you and me going to Rome?

SANT   I'll tell ye in a minute. Now the F.R.S. are sending a deputation to the Vatican to demand certain safeguards for Protestants in the light of the aforesaid recent events, and I'm heading that deputation.

MRS. CROWE   Oh!

SANT   "Sing and rejoice, O daughter of Zion: for, lo, I come, and I will dwell in the midst of thee, saith the Lord."

MRS. CROWE (*impressed*)   Oh, I say.

SANT   Now, you'll be asking yourself—and rightly—why I'm inviting you to come with me, and I wouldn't insult your intelligence by trying to pretend it was just for business reasons only . . . Here, where's your glass?

(*He fills their two glasses again.*)

MRS. CROWE   Not another.

(SANT *refills both glasses and* MRS. CROWE *accepts without further demur.*)

SANT   As leader of this deputation I said to myself who knows your man the Pope better than I do? Why, Nancy Crowe, of course, and she shall come with me.

MRS. CROWE *(impressed and delighted)*   Oh, I say!

SANT   So what do you say?

MRS. CROWE   What could I possibly say, Jerry?

SANT   You can and shall say "Yes," sweetheart. *(He raises his glass.)* Here's to us.

MRS. CROWE   Oh, Jerry! *(They clink glasses.)* Oh, it is nice to see you again, I must say. *(She begins to look soulful.)* Things haven't been too easy for me, one way and another.

SANT   Aye, I suspected as much when I came. And I wouldn't be surprised if it were something to do with that agent of the Whore of Babylon, the erstwhile Baron Corvo, eh?

(MRS. CROWE *does not reply, but consoles herself with another drink.*)

SANT   I'm right, Nancy, aren't I?

(MRS. CROWE *nods her head.*)

SANT   That little barmstick! And I'll wager he hasn't paid you the rent—sneaking out of the house the way he did.

MRS. CROWE *(getting maudlin)* And not even a line to say he'd got there safely. Not even a postcard.

(She starts to snivel.)

SANT Aye. Well, we'll soon get even with him. *(He moves back to his seat beside her, and puts his arm round her shoulders.)* Now a little earlier you were going to tell me something. Now's the time. Come on, Nance.

MRS. CROWE No, I couldn't Jerry. *(She snivels.)*

SANT *(getting tough)* Now, Nancy, you can and you shall tell me.

MRS. CROWE *(content that the moment has come to give in)* Oh, Jerry, it's been going on for years. He—he wouldn't leave me alone, never. He was always—always trying to—to interfere with me, even when Mr. Crowe was alive. I've had no peace whenever he was around, Jerry, and I—I just couldn't keep him away.

(She turns and buries her head in SANT'S *shoulder, sobbing.)*

SANT *(surprised)* Well I'll be damned!

MRS. CROWE Well don't sound so surprised. Aren't I attractive any more?

SANT No, no, of course I'm not surprised, sweetheart. It's just that I always thought—anyway—I'll not stand for a respectable Protestant lady being defiled by a Papish traitor, no matter who. If I had my way I'd geld the lot of them.

MRS. CROWE *(quietly and viciously)* Make him squirm.

    *(*SANT *kisses her violently on the mouth as the lights fade to a*

    BLACKOUT.)

SCENE TWO

An audience chamber in the Vatican.

The only furniture is the pontifical throne, which is set C, on a small dais.

As the lights come up, CARDINAL RAGNA, *Secretary of State, an elderly, bull-like Italian,* CARDINAL BERSTEIN, *a cold, arrogant German, and* FATHER ST. ALBANS, *Prepositor-General of Jesuits, the truculent "Black Pope," an Englishman, enter together from up R and move down C.* RAGNA *is C, with* BERSTEIN *to R and* ST. ALBANS *to L of him.*

ST. ALBANS To a great extent I blame myself. I should have known what a formidable politician my compatriot, Dr. Courtleigh, was.

RAGNA Do not tell me what is a politician. I am Secretary of State. I know what is a politician.

ST. ALBANS *(drily)* Do you? A pity you didn't tumble to his trick earlier then.

BERSTEIN He is crafty like a fox, your English Cardinal.

ST. ALBANS *(sarcastic)* He had seen the light, he said—

RAGNA Ha!

ST. ALBANS —while shaving!

BERSTEIN Ha!

ST. ALBANS We must search afresh, he said. We must search outside the Vatican, he said, for a man of Faith and Constancy, a man of Simplicity and Humility—he said—

RAGNA *(grieving)* Ay, ay, ay!

BERSTEIN A disaster!

RAGNA Catastrophe!

ST. ALBANS Yes, it was a trifle unfortunate.

BERSTEIN Psst! My lords, now that it is all over I am able to reveal to you a matter of great interest.

ST. ALBANS Yes?

BERSTEIN *(proudly)* His Imperial Majesty, the Kaiser, made it known that it was his personal wish that *I* should become the successor to His late Holiness.

ST. ALBANS Oh, really. Well I can reveal to you that the Imperial Kaiser's royal uncle, King Edward, wouldn't have been so stupid as to meddle in matters that didn't concern him.

RAGNA And I am able to reveal to you that your German Kaiser does not know the rules of our Roman Consistory.

If he did, he would know that you, as one of the nine Cardinals-Compromissory, were never eligible for election.

(BERSTEIN *looks put out.*)

RAGNA   But I will make a confession to you, My Lords. Because I thought the election of this one so improbable, I cast my vote for him, *si,* I voted for him in order to— how do you say—to throw away my vote.

BERSTEIN   Oh, really? Frankly, so did I.

(ST. ALBANS *starts a fit of suppressed giggles. The other two stare at him in amazement.*)

BERSTEIN   What is it?

ST. ALBANS   Well, according to Percy van Kristen, so did Vivdi, Cacciatori and old Gintilotto. And you still think that the Archbishop of Pimlico is not an adroit politician?

BERSTEIN   It is true that he succeeded in getting this— this—

ST. ALBANS   Parvenu?

BERSTEIN   This parvenu elected Pope. But what I want to know is how.

ST. ALBANS   Any minute now someone is going to say it is the hand of God.

(RAGNA *and* BERSTEIN *give* ST. ALBANS *a sharp look.*)

RAGNA   The question is not *how* but *why* ... why, why, why?

BERSTEIN *Ja*, why?

ST. ALBANS It could be that Cardinal Courtleigh has a perfectly disinterested reason for placing this bomb under the skirts of *(he gestures with his hand)* you Curia diehards. *(*RAGNA *and* BERSTEIN *look affronted.)* He may feel that some of you lack the simplicity and humility to accede to the Throne of Peter.

BERSTEIN *(nettled)* So he has so much humility, this man?

RAGNA He has the humility of a Neapolitan tenor. You remember at the Coronation when the Cardinal-Archdeacon say, "Holiness what is the Pontifical name you will choose?" he say, "Hadrian the Seventh." I said to him— you heard me, no?—"Your Holiness would perhaps prefer to be called Leo, or Pius, or Gregory, as in the modern manner." But he say—

ST. ALBANS *(imitating* ROLFE*)* "The first and previous English Pontiff was Hadrian the Fourth: the second and present English Pontiff is Hadrian the Seventh. It pleases us: and so by Our Own impulse, We command."

RAGNA *(in disgust)* "By Our Own impulse We command." Such arrogance! Eh! But you heard what he said to me when I tell him it is very—*pericoloso*—

ST. ALBANS Dangerous.

RAGNA —dangerous to walk to Lateran? I said for the Holy Father to walk to Lateran through the streets of Rome today is madness.

ST. ALBANS Why? It's only about half a mile, isn't it?

RAGNA You English do not understand. Rome is not your Tunbridge or Cheltenham Spa. The city is full of Jews and Freemasons.

ST. ALBANS So is Cheltenham Spa.

RAGNA They will throw vitriol at us. It is suicide for you, and is murder for me.

ST. ALBANS And what did he say?

RAGNA He say, "Good. The Church is badly wanting a new martyr."

> (ST. ALBANS *and* BERSTEIN *also move L,* ST. ALBANS *suppressing laughter,* BERSTEIN *tut-tutting.* COURT-LEIGH, TALACRYN *and other members of the Sacred College enter up R.* COURTLEIGH *is wheeled on in a bathchair, to down RC.* TALACRYN *also moves RC. The others form a semi-circle on either side of the throne, which remains vacant.)*

COURTLEIGH Can anyone enlighten me as to the reason for this hasty summons?

RAGNA *(with a gesture of resignation)* Ecco!

COURTLEIGH Had to gobble me breakfast. Haven't even had a chance to read the *Times* yet.

ST. ALBANS Your Eminence could hardly have done so.

COURTLEIGH What do you mean?

ST. ALBANS   I am informed that an embargo has been placed on all newspapers within the Vatican.

COURTLEIGH   Extraordinary!

ST. ALBANS   However, I made it my business to find out the reason for this, and it appears that the embargo was placed by His Holiness prior to the publication of his Bull and Breve.

> *(There are exclamations of astonishment from several CARDINALS.)*

ST. ALBANS   Further, I made it my business to obtain a copy of the text of this Bull and Breve and I think Your Eminences will be interested if I read it to you.

> *(More exclamations. ST. ALBANS clears his throat and pauses for effect. He then reads from a sheet of paper. The CARDINALS stop muttering.)*

ST. ALBANS   "We, Hadrian the Seventh, Vicar of Christ, Servant of the servants of God, speak thus: We find Ourselves the sovereign of an estate to which We hold no title deeds. But Our Kingdom is not of this world. So, therefore, We, Vicar of Christ, Successor to the Throne of St. Peter, do now make Our formal and unconditional renunciation to temporal Sovereignty."

> *(The CARDINALS gasp.)*

ST. ALBANS   "Our predecessors followed other counsels and they acted in the knowledge of their responsibility to God. We, on Our part, act as We deem best. We are

God's Vice-regent and this is Our will. *(Quickly)* Given at Rome, at St. Peter's by the Vatican, on this day of Our Supreme Pontificate."

(There is a moment of utter silence.)

RAGNA *(shouting)*   Judas! Judas! This shall not be!

ST. ALBANS   Unfortunately, Lord Cardinal, it can be—and is.

RAGNA   Am I Secretary of State or am I not Secretary of State? I am asking Your Eminences. If the Pontiff is no longer temporal sovereign, how am I Secretary of the Vatican State? You tell me I am to be dismissed by this—this clerk who has the sack from two—not one, but two—ecclesiastical colleges?

BERSTEIN   Two colleges! *(He tut-tuts.)*

TALACRYN   His Holiness believes the world is sick for want of the Church. He believes, I think, that we should turn all our efforts and attention to the pursuit of non-secular matters.

RAGNA *(striding R and back to L)*   *Va bene, va bene.* But I tell you His Holiness has very special conception of His Apostolic character. He think that is enough. It is not enough.

BERSTEIN   *Ja, ja.* It is not enough. If the temporal power is worth having, it is worth fighting for.

ST. ALBANS   I do not say that I disagree with Your Eminence.

67

RAGNA   Then perhaps you will make a suggestion. You say Jesuits are always very clever. Why do you not suggest we convene the Oecumenical Council? Eh?

BERSTEIN   *Ja, ja.* The Oecumenical Council only can deal with such matters.

RAGNA   I say this man is a heretic. I say he is the Anti-Pope. And I say the Sacred College must act now—before it is too late.

ST. ALBANS   And I wouldn't necessarily argue with Your Eminence, but the Oecumenical Council of the Vatican has stood adjourned since—I think I am right in saying —since eighteen-seventy. All the same . . .

RAGNA   But all the same it can be reconvened, no?

BERSTEIN   Under the circumstances it is the only thing to do. I agree.

ST. ALBANS   If the Sacred College should choose to demand . . .

RAGNA   *(roaring)*   The Sacred College *should* demand.

(Unnoticed, HADRIAN [ROLFE] *enters quietly from up R. For the first time he is seen wearing the white garments of a Pope. He carries a large leather folder.)*

RAGNA   If there's any anxiety or doubt in any minds the Sacred College *must* demand.

HADRIAN   *(moving R of the throne: very quietly)*   Pray, what must the Sacred College demand, Lord Cardinal?

(All react to the sudden appearance of the POPE. RAGNA, *taken off guard, can only work his jaw defiantly.* HADRIAN *persists in his most ominously gentle voice.)*

HADRIAN   Your Eminence is free to address Us.

RAGNA *(recovering his truculence slightly)*   I wish rather to address the Sacred College.

HADRIAN *(sweetly)*   You have Our permission to do so.

(He looks round the room, noting the reactions of those present.)

RAGNA *(moving L of the throne)*   I wish to—*(He clears his throat to gain time.)* I wish to . . .

HADRIAN   You wish to denounce Us as Heretic and Pseudo-Pontiff. And to do so, you wish to convene an Oecumenical Council. Is that not correct?

*(*RAGNA, *his own words taken from his mouth, remains silent, his face working.)*

HADRIAN   That generally is done by oblique-eyed Cardinals who cannot accustom themselves to new Pontiffs. *(Mounting the dais)* But Lord Cardinals, if such an idea should be presented to you, be ye mindful that none but the Supreme Pontiff can convoke an Oecumenical Council. We are conscious of your love and of your loathing for Our Person and Our Acts. We value the one and regret the other. But ye voluntarily have sworn obedience to Us, and We claim it. Nothing must and nothing shall obstruct Us. Let that be known. *(He sits on the throne.)*

Wherefore Most Eminent Lords and Venerable Fathers, let not the sheep of Christ's flock be neglected while the shepherds exchange anathemas. Try, Venerable Fathers, to believe that the time has come for taking stock. Ask yourselves whether we really are as successful as we think we are—whether in fact we are not abject and lamentable failures in the eyes of God. We have added and added to the riches, pomp and power of the Church, yet everywhere there is great wealth alongside dire poverty; there are strong nations brutally holding small ones to slavery; above all there are millions of people of goodwill looking to us for moral and spiritual leadership who get from us only dogmatic interpretations of canon law in return. If, then, we have so far failed in spreading Christ's Gospel, let us try anew. Let us try the road of Apostolic simplicity —the simplicity of Peter the Fisherman. At least let us try.

(There is total silence.)

HADRIAN   Your Eminences have permission to retire.

(For a moment there is silence. Then TALACRYN *goes quickly to re-affirm his allegiance by kissing the Pontifical ring. Hesitantly at first, the others follow.* RAGNA, *still recalcitrant, makes the briefest possible acknowledgement.* COURTLEIGH *alone is left, in his chair. Having made obeisance, the prelates move off up R, murmuring.)*

HADRIAN *(to* COURTLEIGH*)*   We should be glad if Your Eminence could spare a few moments longer of your time.

COURTLEIGH *(coolly)*   I am at Your Holiness's disposal. I pray Your Holiness will forgive this chair.

HADRIAN   We trust Your Eminence is not seriously incommoded.

COURTLEIGH   A very English complaint, Holy Father, a touch of the gout.

HADRIAN   Accept Our sympathy for your English complaint. We too have them, but of a different nature. We desire to establish relations with Your Eminence, chiefly because you hold so responsible a position in England, a country dear above all others to Us.

COURTLEIGH *(putting on his cardinalatial mask expressive of the old and wise condescending to give ear to the young and rash)*   Proceed, Most Holy Father.

HADRIAN   It is Our wish to make England's people prepared for the Lord. But we find Ourselves impeded at the outset by the present conduct of the English Roman Catholics—especially of the aboriginal English Catholics.

> (COURTLEIGH *reacts sharply, then bows slightly and continues to attend.*
>
>   HADRIAN *opens his folder, which contains press cuttings.)*

HADRIAN   Kindly give Us your opinion of this statement, Eminence. I quote from a London newspaper whose views are not necessarily our own. "The Roman Catholic laity resident in England are petitioning Parliament to set up some control over Roman Catholic monies and interests. It is alleged that no account is afforded by the Roman Catholic Bishops of the management or disbursement of such properties and monies." Well?

COURTLEIGH   The scandal emanated from a priest not of my Archdiocese, Holiness. We were successful in preventing it from spreading.

HADRIAN   Oh! Then there was such a petition? I was prepared to ascribe it to the imagination of one of the bright young men usually employed by the monstrous old proprietor of this newspaper. And were there many supporters of the petition?

COURTLEIGH *(raising a hand)*   Unfortunately, there were a number.

HADRIAN   And were there any grounds for the allegations?

COURTLEIGH   Holy Father, we cannot be expected to account to every Tom, Dick and Harry for the hundreds of bequests and endowments which we administer.

HADRIAN   Why not, if your accounts are properly audited? We assume they are?

COURTLEIGH   Ah—to a great extent, yes.

HADRIAN   To a great extent? Not invariably? But do you really consider your clergy capable of financial administration?

COURTLEIGH   As capable as other men.

HADRIAN   Priests are not "as other men."

COURTLEIGH   But what would Your Holiness have?

HADRIAN   We entirely disapprove of the clergy using any

72

secular power whatever, especially such power as inheres in the command of money. The clergy are ministers—ministers—not masters. The clergy are *more*, not *less*, human, and they certainly are not the pick of humanity.

COURTLEIGH   Even if I were to agree, I still do not precisely see Your Holiness's point.

HADRIAN   No? Then let us take another. *(He rises and moves LC, taking a small green ticket from the folder.)* This does come from Your Eminence's diocese. "Church of the Sacred Heart—admit bearer to Midnight Mass—Christmas Eve—Middle Seat one shilling and sixpence." Surely not some form of discrimination?

COURTLEIGH   *(shrugging, as if the card were of no significance)*   A small attempt to prevent—ah—improper persons from attending these services.

HADRIAN   But "improper" persons should be encouraged to attend.

COURTLEIGH   *(irritated)*   And have scenes of disorder and profanation?

HADRIAN   We are determined that Our Churches be made as free to the lost as to the saved.

COURTLEIGH   May I be permitted to ask what experience Your Holiness has had in parochial administration?

HADRIAN   You could answer that question yourself, Your Eminence. But I've attended many midnight masses and heard no sign of the profanation of which you speak. Sots and harlots were undoubtedly present, but they were not disorderly. They were cowed, they were sleepy, they were curious, but they made no noise. If means of grace are obtainable in a Church, who dare deny them to those who need them most? You are here to serve—and only to serve. We especially disapprove of any system which makes access to the Church difficult—like this admission fee.

COURTLEIGH   Holy Father, the clergy must live.

HADRIAN   And so they shall. But pew-rents are abominable —and so are pews. Abolish them both.

COURTLEIGH   *(beside himself with rage)*   Your Holiness speaks as though He was not one of us.

(HADRIAN *pauses and fixes* COURTLEIGH *with a look.*)

HADRIAN   Look at your Catholic Directory and see the advertisement of a priest who is prepared to pay bank interest on investments—in plain words borrow money upon usury, in direct contravention to St. Luke. Look at the Catholic Hour and see the advertisement of a priest who actually trades as a tobacconist. Look in the precincts of your churches and see the tables of the Fenian literature sellers and the seats of them that sell tickets for stage plays and bazaars. No, My Lord Cardinal, the clergy attempt too much. They may be excellent priests, but as tradesmen, stock jobbers and variety entertainers, they are catastrophes.

COURTLEIGH   *(with resignation)*   But Holy Father, do think for a moment. What are the clergy to live on?

HADRIAN   The free-will offerings of the faithful.

COURTLEIGH   But suppose the faithful do not give of their free will?

HADRIAN   Then starve and go to heaven.

COURTLEIGH   *(stung once more to defend himself)*   Your Holiness will permit me to remind you that I, myself, was consecrated bishop fourteen years before you were made a Christian at baptism. It seems to me that you should give your seniors credit for having consciences of their own.

HADRIAN   *(circling slowly below* COURTLEIGH's *chair, above it, behind the throne, and L of it to C)*   My dear Lord Cardinal, if We had seen the least sign of the said consciences . . .

COURTLEIGH   I am not the only member of the Sacred College who thinks that Your Holiness's attitude partakes of —singularity—and—ah—arrogance.

HADRIAN   Singularity? Oh, We sincerely hope so. But arrogance—We cannot call it arrogance that We have attempted to show you something of Our frame of mind.

COURTLEIGH   What, then, Holy Father, would You wish me to do?

HADRIAN   We wish you to act upon the sum of Our words and conduct in order that England may have a good, and not a bad, example from English Catholics. No more than that. The Barque of Peter is way off course. Lord Cardi-

nal, can the new Captain count on the loyal support of
His Lieutenant in trying to bring her head round?

COURTLEIGH *(making an immense effort)* Holy Father, I
assure you that You may count on me.

HADRIAN We realize the immense effort on your part that
has made you give Us this assurance and it gladdens Us
to see this evidence of the Grace of your Divine Vocation.

(COURTLEIGH bows slightly.)

HADRIAN Well now, Lord Cardinal, to change the metaphor,
let us put away the flail and take up the crook. So shall we
take a little stroll in the garden and say some Office?

COURTLEIGH *(surprised)* Oh, well, certainly, with pleasure
—that is if Your Holiness doesn't mind walking by the
side of my bathchair, that is . . .

HADRIAN Oh, but We do. It is Our invariable custom to
walk *behind* bathchairs and push them.

COURTLEIGH Oh but, Holy Father, I could not for one moment permit . . .

HADRIAN No, but for just one hour you will submit.

COURTLEIGH All the same, Holy Father, really . . .

HADRIAN *(putting his folder on* COURTLEIGH'*s lap and moving
behind the bathchair)* Nonsense man, do you suppose
that One has never pushed a bathchair before?

COURTLEIGH   All the same, Holy Father, it is hardly . . .

HADRIAN   Now sit quietly and open your breviary and start reading the Office.

(COURTLEIGH *obeys.*)

HADRIAN   We will look over your shoulder and make the responses. *(He swivels the bathchair round.)* It's awfully good exercise, you know.

(*Respectively saying and responding to the office of the day,* HADRIAN *pushes the aged* COURTLEIGH *slowly off up R, as the lights fade to a*

BLACKOUT.)

SCENE THREE

Outside a café in Rome.

 A table and two chairs are set down L.

 When the lights come up, SANT *and* MRS. CROWE *are
sitting at the table, which is outside the café.* MRS. CROWE,
seated L, is shielding herself with a parasol. SANT, *R, fans
himself with a panama hat. He holds a piece of paper in his
other hand.*

SANT This is my ultimatum. Listen. *(He reads.)* "Since my
earlier communication in which I had the pleasure of addressing you on the aims of the Fellowship of Religious
Segregation, I have been anxiously waiting the favour of
an acknowledgement of same. In case the subject has
slipped your memory, I should remind you that we were
not adverse to give our careful consideration to any pro-
posal you may see fit to make, financial or otherwise."
That's putting it fair and square, eh?

MRS. CROWE Yes, Jerry, but how's he going to know that
you want to talk to him about the other—you know . . .

SANT Hold your horses, woman, I haven't come to the guts
of it yet. *(Continuing to read)* "But I am quite at a loss

to understand on what grounds you have not yet favoured me with a reply unless there is anything on which you would like further explanation. In which case, I will be most happy to call on you per appointment for which I have been waiting at the above address here in Rome for some weeks and neglecting my business at considerable expense and inconvenience which a man in my position cannot be expected to incur and common courtesy demands should be made good."

(The lights fade to a

BLACKOUT.*)*

SCENE FOUR

The audience chamber.

As the lights come up, TALACRYN *and* HADRIAN *are entering up* R. TALACRYN *is reading the remainder of* SANT'S *letter.* HADRIAN *is smoking a home-rolled cigarette. He moves to the throne and sits still and tense as* TALACRYN *reads.*

TALACRYN   "... should be made good. I therefore trust that in view of the not altogether pleasant facts that are in the possession of myself and another party well known to yourself, you will see fit to accord me a private interview at your earliest convenience. Hoping that I will not ..."

(HADRIAN *remains rigid. His hand trembles as he removes his cigarette.*)

HADRIAN   Stop! I cannot bring myself to hear any more of that illiterate filth.

TALACRYN   Forgive the presumption, but Your Holiness seems unduly upset by this impertinent nonsense.

HADRIAN   It is not His Holiness who is upset, but Frederick William Rolfe.

TALACRYN   Again forgive the presumption, but one has known Frederick William Rolfe for some years. Who are these enemies, Holy Father?

HADRIAN   Prurient scum. Pithycanthropoids and Neanderthals who beset Our path in Our previous and ghastly existence.

TALACRYN   They can be annihilated, Holiness. Surely some guillotine can be brought down that would effectively silence these . . .

HADRIAN   Blackmailers? Since Our conscience is clear, We have no desire to be so dynamic. We should not touch ordure even with a shovel.

TALACRYN   But silence is more likely to inflame such people than to quiet them. Supposing in their frustration they go to the newspapers?

HADRIAN   Then, doubtless, the Sacred College will erect their tail feathers and gobble like a flock of huge turkeycocks: "Behold the Anti-Pope!" they will say, and glare whole Inquisitions at us.

TALACRYN   Respectfully, Holiness, the matter should not be allowed to reach such a pass. As Your Holiness rightly assumes, those within the Sacred College who were against Your accession would welcome a scandal directed at Your Person.

HADRIAN   Let them have a scandal. Let them keep aloof in their vermilion sulks. It is not Our will to move in this matter.

TALACRYN   But, forgive me if I persist, Holiness . . .

HADRIAN *(sharply)*   Do not persist. *(He rises and moves LC, putting out his cigarette with his foot. Changing from the Pontifical to the familiar)* Frank, tell me, what have you been doing today?

TALACRYN   Today? Oh, I paid a visit, as a matter of fact, to Your old college.

HADRIAN *(freezing)*   Oh?

TALACRYN   They cannot understand why You have not yet been to see them.

HADRIAN   Is not the Rector still the same man who once expelled me—brutally and without explanation?

TALACRYN   The Rector is an old man now, sensible to the errors of his youth, as we all are.

HADRIAN *(to himself)*   The wound goes deep. It has never properly healed.

TALACRYN   Perhaps this is the moment for cauterizing the wound, Holiness. Strangely, I forgot the horrors of my own times there after I'd visited them once or twice. Besides, the young men love to see one, and the older men —the principals—like to see the hierarchy take note of them.

HADRIAN *(suddenly moving to* TALACRYN*)*   Frank, let's go to the college now. We can get there in time for lunch?

TALACRYN *(looking pleased)* What a good idea.

(As TALACRYN *and* HADRIAN *move quickly upstage, the lights fade to a*

BLACKOUT.*)*

SCENE FIVE

The college.

The stage is bare.

As the lights come up we hear a distant bell, and a distant litany being chanted. Some young SEMINARISTS *in purple sopranos pass across from up R to up L, singing. Among them is* ROSE. *When they have passed from sight,* HADRIAN *enters R with* TALACRYN *and the* RECTOR. *The* RECTOR, *dressed in black, is an old man whose behaviour before the* POPE *is a mixture of self-importance and obsequiousness—the headmaster humouring a distinguished parent. The three men move C, the* RECTOR *between* HADRIAN, *L, and* TALACRYN, *R.*

RECTOR   This has been a great day for the College, Holy Father.

*(*HADRIAN *ignores the flattery.)*

RECTOR   Of course, had we known Your Holiness intended to honour us, a proper reception . . .

HADRIAN   Quite unnecessary. Our children expect to see Us and We came to be seen. We now wish to know something of one student in particular.

RECTOR   Who is that, Holy Father?

HADRIAN   The somewhat older man who looks so hungry and took only bread and water at luncheon.

RECTOR   Ah, poor fellow!

HADRIAN   Now why do you say that, Monsignore?

RECTOR   Well, Holiness, I'm afraid this is not the place for him. He's very sensitive and doesn't really get on with the others.

HADRIAN   Does he quarrel with them?

RECTOR   Oh no. But he takes pains to avoid them.

HADRIAN   Perhaps he has his reasons.

RECTOR   Perhaps, but his attitude does not seem suitable in one hoping to attain Orders! He is not what I would call a good mixer.

HADRIAN   You talk as if he aspired to be a sporting parson.

RECTOR *(nettled)*   I must tell Your Holiness that I do not feel that he has a real Vocation for the priesthood.

HADRIAN   Please know, Monsignore, that We have not come here to brag or to gloat, but we feel bound to remind you that your judgement as to vocation has, in the past, been in error.

RECTOR *(shaken)*   I am only too mindful—Your Holiness's

personal case has for a long time been—it was a long time ago. I can only say in extenuation that to err is human.

HADRIAN *(crossing below the others to R)*   Human error is sometimes excusable. *In*human behaviour is not. Ill-considered judgement by those in authority are damnably culpable.

> *(The* RECTOR *winces.)*

HADRIAN   What is the name of this student who has "no Vocation"?

RECTOR   Rose, Holiness. George Arthur Rose.

HADRIAN   We wish to speak to him.

RECTOR   If it pleases Your Holiness.

HADRIAN   We will speak to him alone.

> *(The* RECTOR *bows and exits up R.)*

HADRIAN *(to* TALACRYN, *when they are alone)*   Were We too severe, Frank? The wish to smoke has made Us irritable.

TALACRYN *(smiling)*   Your Holiness was altogether admirable. I must admit to having enjoyed the last five minutes more than a Christian should.

> *(During the following speeches* HADRIAN *and* TALA-
> CRYN *stroll up and down L.)*

HADRIAN *(looking round and sniffing)* Still the same smell. The inevitable odour of hot boy.

TALACRYN It seems to be the inescapable adjunct of education.

HADRIAN Inescapable? Nonsense! We have half a mind to appoint you Protector of this College. Yes, that's right. You will give them sanitation—and sanity, for goodness sake. You might make that shrubbery into a gymnasium. And what about a swimming pool—with a lovely terrace on the top?

TALACRYN I don't see why not.

HADRIAN And, Frank, make friends with them and see what you can do to take that horrible secretive suppressed look out of their young eyes. You understand?

TALACRYN I think so, Holiness.

(The RECTOR *enters up R with* ROSE, *who is dressed in the violet cassock and black soprano of a seminarist.)*

RECTOR Mr. Rose, Your Holiness.

*(*ROSE *observes the forms, and moves to C.)*

HADRIAN You will be pleased to hear, Monsignore, that We have appointed the Bishop of Caerleon Protector of St. Andrew's College. His Lordship would be most grateful if you would now take him on a detailed tour of the kitchens and sanitary arrangements.

(The RECTOR *looks surprised, but is now totally submissive.)*

RECTOR   As Your Holiness pleases.

(The RECTOR *and* TALACRYN *exit up R.* ROSE *does not show surprise but stands up C throughout with dignity and reserve.)*

HADRIAN *(moving R of* ROSE*)*   Dear son, on slight knowledge We have the impression you are one of the unhappy ones. Will you confide in Us?

ROSE   I have not complained, Sanctity.

HADRIAN   But now you may do so.

ROSE   I have no reason—I do not wish to do so.

HADRIAN   How old are you, my son?

ROSE   Twenty-nine, Sanctity.

HADRIAN   And you find your environment disagreeable?

ROSE   All environments are more or less disagreeable to me.

HADRIAN   Up to the present at least. You find that your circumstances adversely influence your conduct—prevent you from doing yourself justice—here.

ROSE   That may be my fault.

HADRIAN   They mock you, no doubt.

ROSE I suppose that is the case, Holiness.

HADRIAN So was Jesus Christ mocked. But why are you?

ROSE Because for my ablutions I carry two cans of water up two hundred and two steps every day.

HADRIAN No doubt they say you must be a very unclean person to need so much washing.

ROSE Sanctity, you are quoting the Rector.

HADRIAN No.

ROSE How does Your Holiness know so exactly?

HADRIAN *(laughing)* Have they even put a snake in your water cans?

ROSE No, they have not done that.

HADRIAN They did in Ours. Isn't it absurd?

ROSE It is—and very disconcerting.

HADRIAN But you try not to let it disconcert you?

ROSE I try but I fail. My heart is always on my sleeve and the daws peck it. So I try to protect myself in isolation.

HADRIAN That they call "sulkiness"!

ROSE Yes, Your Holiness knows so exactly . . .

HADRIAN *(moving slowly upstage: almost to himself)* We

also were never able to arrange to be loved. *(He circles slowly above* ROSE *and down to LC.)* Do you always live on bread and water?

ROSE   Yes, except for eggs.

HADRIAN   Eggs? Why eggs?

ROSE   I have been into the kitchen and seen—things. They cannot deposit sputum inside the shells of boiled eggs.

HADRIAN *(moving across the stage to down R)*   Do you like bread and water?

ROSE   No, but in order not to be singular I eat and drink what I can of what is set before me. But because of that, I am deemed more singular than ever.

HADRIAN *(moving round above* ROSE *to LC as before)*   Yet you choose to persevere, my son!

ROSE   Sanctity, I must. I am called.

HADRIAN   You are sure of that?

ROSE   It is the only thing in all the world of which I am sure.

HADRIAN   Yet you know that this college is not the place for you?

ROSE   I suppose not. But my diocesan sent me here and I intend to serve my sentence.

HADRIAN   Dear son, what is your ambition?

ROSE   Priesthood.

HADRIAN   And you *will* persevere—for however long?

ROSE   For twenty years if need be.

HADRIAN   We persevered for just that length of time.

ROSE   Then so will I.

HADRIAN   My son, it is in Our power to grant you a favour. Do you wish to ask Us for anything?

ROSE   No thank you, Sanctity.

HADRIAN   My son, do you think you are ready for priesthood?

ROSE   I am ready as soon as I may be summoned, Sanctity.

HADRIAN   You shall be summoned. Come to Vatican tomorrow and ask for the Bishop of Caerleon. He will expect you. Your desire may soon be fulfilled. Will you pray for Us, dear son?

ROSE   Holy Father, I most surely will.

HADRIAN   Good-bye, and God bless you.

> (ROSE *kneels and* HADRIAN *gives blessing.*
> ROSE *exits R and* HADRIAN *moves down L.*
> TALACRYN *and the* RECTOR *enter up L. The* RECTOR *crosses and exits up R.* TALACRYN *moves downstage to* HADRIAN.)

HADRIAN   What a delicious day it has been, Frank. You persuaded Us and We are grateful.

TALACRYN   I think the walk did Your Holiness good.

HADRIAN   It was not just the walk, but something quite other—as though a curtain has been lifted, or, more exactly, as if We had been given a brief glimpse into a human heart.

TALACRYN   That is a rare and wonderful experience, Holiness.

HADRIAN   Rare? You are Our confessor. You must know that for Us the experience is unique. Frank, We have just had the first feeling of undiluted enjoyment of human society which We can ever remember.

TALACRYN   Do you remember what I said to you in London, Holiness? I said that if You could find it in Yourself to love your neighbour it would lead You to love God.

HADRIAN   Love—yes—We have recognized for the first time in Ourselves a new and unborn power, a perfectly strange capability. Today, We have made experience of a feeling which—well, which We suppose—at any rate will pass for—Love.

(As they move up R the lights fade to a

BLACKOUT*.)*

SCENE SIX

The audience chamber.

A small chair has been set down RC, facing towards the throne.

When the lights come up, AGNES *is discovered sitting on the chair RC looking very nervous.* FATHER ROSE, *now in the cassock of an ordained priest, enters up L. He has a clip of papers in his hand.*

FR. ROSE   Mrs. Agnes Dixon?

AGNES   Yers?

FR. ROSE   His Holiness asked me to convey his apologies to you. He has been slightly delayed.

AGNES   That's quite all right, dear, ta.

>   (FR. ROSE *nods and moves L of the throne. There is an awkward silence as they both wait for* HADRIAN.)

AGNES   Been keeping busy then?

FR. ROSE *(slightly taken aback)*   Well, as a private chaplain to His Holiness I find the days full.

AGNES   I daresay you do. He's a handful all right. When I
used to look after him myself . . .

(Further conversation is prevented by the entrance of
HADRIAN *up L.)*

FR. ROSE   Mrs. Agnes Dixon, Your Holiness.

*(*AGNES *rises, trots to C and flops on her knees.*
HADRIAN *immediately attempts to assist her to rise.)*

HADRIAN   Agnes.

AGNES   Oooh, my joints!

HADRIAN *(throwing off completely his cold pontifical manner)*
Agnes, please sit down.

AGNES   I don't mind, sir.

HADRIAN *(moving her chair R of the throne)*   Please, Agnes,
here.

AGNES *(sitting)*   Oooh, that's better. I've been on my feet
all day, and don't these marble floors tell.

HADRIAN *(sitting on the throne)*   I'm sorry, Agnes.

AGNES   I shouldn't be saying such things, should I, not now
with you living here.

HADRIAN   Good friends are few, Agnes—particularly in the
Vatican.

AGNES   These your chairs, are they?

HADRIAN   Well, I suppose they go with the job.

AGNES   Not very comfy, are they? Still—oh, there I am again! But there, I can't help but think of you still as Mr. Rolfe I used to do for.

HADRIAN   It's good to hear you say so, Agnes.

AGNES   *(scrabbling in her capacious bag and bringing forth a packet)*   Here we are, then.

HADRIAN   *(taking it)*   What is this?

AGNES   Why, the change, of course.

HADRIAN   Change?

AGNES   From the money you sent me to buy that house. I got it cheaper than we thought because it'd been empty so long.

HADRIAN   Oh, but you dear good soul, I didn't expect any change. It's all yours. Besides, you may need it to tide you over till you get the lodgers.

AGNES   Till I can get the lodgers? Why, I'm turning them away already. *(She dives in her bag again.)* Oh, I nearly forgot, what with all the excitement and walking along those stone corridors with those gentlemen in their fancy get-up. One of them was ever so stuck-up, he was. I couldn't help saying, "I seen plenty more like you, my lad, at the old Holborn Empire." Oh yes, I did, but I don't think he knew what I meant. There, I knew I had it some-where. *(She produces a jar of pickles.)* It's the pickles you always had a fancy for. Made just the same as I used to. You always had a tooth for them, didn't you?

HADRIAN   Dear, good Agnes, you're kindness itself. You know, I never get anything like this nowadays. George, try one.

> *(All three help themselves to a pickled onion.* FR. ROSE *gallantly tries to conceal his dislike. There is a long pause as they all munch.)*

AGNES *(with her mouth full)*   Well, I must say it's good to see you again, sir, for all you've come up in the world. All the same, I shall never get used to your being Pope, never. Oh, I hope you don't think I don't know my place!

HADRIAN *(rising)*   Your place, Agnes, is always close to Our heart.

AGNES *(rising)*   Well, I mustn't detain you, Mr. Rolfe, so I'll be getting along just as soon as you give me a blessing and say a bit of a prayer. Thank you, sir, for all you've done and I'll say a prayer for you every day for as long as I'm spared.

> *(*AGNES *gets, with some difficulty, to her knees and receives the Pontifical blessing.)*

HADRIAN *(causing her to rise)*   Are you going back at once, Agnes?

AGNES   Well, I was thinking of having a bit of a look-round

before going back. It's silly to come all this way and not
see the sights.

HADRIAN *(taking a card and pen from* FR. ROSE*)*   Then take
this card—*(he writes on the card)*—give it to the "fancy
gentleman" who is going to take you downstairs and tell
him what you want to see. Thank you.

AGNES   Will they want me to give the card up at the door?

HADRIAN   Not if you want to keep it.

AGNES   I'll keep this card till I'm laid out. God bless you, my
dear.

> *(She kisses the* POPE's *ring, gets up, not without diffi-
> culty, and moves up R.*
> > FR. ROSE *goes to* AGNES *and they both exit up R.)*

HADRIAN *(moving LC)*   Filthy hypocrite! *(After a pause,
he smiles gently to himself.)*

> *(*TALACRYN *enters with unusual lack of formality. He
> obviously bears urgent news.)*

TALACRYN *(moving quickly down L to* HADRIAN*)*   Forgive
my precipitance, Holiness, but the news I bring—is of the
greatest urgency.

HADRIAN *(still   unconcerned)*   You're   quite   breathless,
Frank. A man of your age must take care. *(He taps his
heart significantly.)*

TALACRYN   Holiness, please let me be serious. Calumnies

have been published. Terrible things have been said.

HADRIAN *(freezing)* Oh? What sort of things? By whom? Who has published them?

TALACRYN Malignant things referring to Your Holiness's secular life. Published in an Ulster newspaper, and worse . . .

HADRIAN Yes?

TALACRYN In a prominent journal sponsored by the Church.

HADRIAN Who has written this? What has been said?

> *(RAGNA swirls in triumphantly up R, bearing a sheaf of newspapers. He moves R of the throne. All the other CARDINALS follow him on and form an arc, some moving RC, others behind the throne to LC.)*

RAGNA Perhaps these will inform Your Holiness.

> *(HADRIAN moves L of the throne and take the papers.)*

RAGNA Your Holiness is well qualified to appreciate the validity of your English newspapers.

> *(HADRIAN starts to read.)*

RAGNA These English newspapers have been to much trouble. Suddenly they find it very interesting to make study of the life of the English Pope. They find very interesting things.

HADRIAN *(still reading: half to himself)* Half-truth.

RAGNA His Holiness was expelled from ecclesiastical college in Rome because he is owing everybody money. He makes friends with old Italian lady, the Duchess of Sforza-Cesarini, who is very rich.

HADRIAN *(to himself)* Unanswerable, because it is half-truth.

RAGNA Back in England, His Holiness becomes "Baron Corvo," a fine gentleman who inherited title from his noble Italian friend. He used title to gain influence and obtain more money.

HADRIAN *(still to himself)* Half-truth again. Who could have attacked with such malign ingenuity?

RAGNA The Baron tries to buy some property, but people find he is not "Baron." He has no money to buy property. He is a fraud, an adventurer.

HADRIAN *(searching the column)* Anonymous! Anonymous half-truths. I should be able to recognize the filthy paw of this muck-raker.

RAGNA So "Baron Corvo" runs away—to another town where he makes more trouble and owes more money; this time in Wales.

HADRIAN We were not in Wales this time—but in Belfast. Yes, of course—Sant! Jeremiah Sant!

RAGNA But in Ireland it is also the same story; he is again

99

the great gentleman—the writer, photographer, inventor of many things, a friend of many famous people. But it is all lies. He has no money. He has no friends. He is nothing. He owes money to the people where he is living. They take him from bed and put him in the street. They throw his clothes after him so he must dress in the street.

(TALACRYN *reacts sharply at this humiliating revelation.)*

HADRIAN *(looking at* RAGNA*)*   Yes. We appear to be a very disreputable character, do We not. But We demand, Lord Cardinal, that you take note of certain errors.

RAGNA   Errors in Your English newspapers?

HADRIAN   Ten, eleven, twelve, thirteen, fourteen, fifteen— why should English newspapers be less corrupt than Italian? Fifteen absolute and deliberate lies, in a column and a half of print. *(He returns the newspapers and sits on the throne.)* Well, Lord Cardinal?

RAGNA *(getting angry)*   Very well, you tell me this is all lies. But today the whole world is reading these papers. What are You going to do?

HADRIAN *(icily)*   We will ponder the matter Your Eminence has set before Us, and at a convenient time We will declare Our pleasure.

RAGNA *(almost apoplectic)*   Convenient time, eh? Let me remind Your Holiness that I am Cardinal Secretary of State of the Vatican, and I demand to know what you are going to do.

*(After an embarrassed pause, there is a general mur-
mur of assent.)*

COURTLEIGH   Holiness, we—that is—many of us feel that
Your Holiness has been grossly misrepresented. We would
appreciate a statement to refute these calumnies by the
press.

HADRIAN *(in a voice of icy reticence)*   Very well. I will give
to the Sacred College that statement. And when I have
finished speaking I never will return to this subject. Gentlemen, would some of you like to put Frederick William
Rolfe to the question.

COURTLEIGH   Then if Your Holiness would enlighten . . .

HADRIAN   There is no Holiness here.

COURTLEIGH *(bowing acknowledgement)*   I must confess
that the question of pseudonyms is of interest.

HADRIAN *(moving upstage to the throne and turning below
it)*   Pseudonyms: when I was kicked out of St. Andrew's
College without a farthing or a friend I was obliged to live
by my wits. Thank God who gave me wits to live by. Think
of this: I was a tonsured clerk forced to earn a living by
secular means, but always intending to persist in my Divine
Vocation. I had a shuddering repugnance from associating
my name, the name by which some day I should be known
in the priesthood, with secular pursuits, so I adopted a
pseudonym. But as time went on and Catholic malfeasance
drove me from one trade to another, I split up my per-
sonality and carried on each trade under a separate pseudonym! Thus as Baron Corvo I wrote and painted and photo-

graphed; as F. Austin I designed decorations; as Frank Hochheimer I did journalism. There were four at least. Four entities careering round like colts in a meadow dissipating energy which, but for the imbecility of the Church, could have been canalized to fulfil its proper purpose years ago.

RAGNA *(tapping the newspapers)* What about the debts? Perhaps you explain the debts, please.

HADRIAN Debts! From the moment they were first contracted with the connivance and consent of certain prelates not unknown to some of you here—

> (COURTLEIGH *and* TALACRYN *show signs of embarrassment.)*

HADRIAN —debts were never off my chest for twenty years. I was foolish enough to believe that you Catholics would keep your promises and pay me for the work which I did at your orders. So I accepted credit. I worked—God knows how I worked—and expected a just wage. When it was withheld, people encouraged me to hope and work on. They offered me the odd guinea to go on with. I took the filthy guinea. God forgive me for becoming so degraded. But one can't pay one's debts and lead a godly life for ever on an occasional guinea. My weakness, my fault was that I did not die—murdered at St. Andrew's College.

> *(He turns away L.)*

BERSTEIN Perhaps you will now condescend to explain the allegations of luxurious living.

COURTLEIGH My Lord Berstein . . .

TALACRYN *(to* HADRIAN*)* Holy Father, don't say another word. *(Turning to his colleagues)* Shame on you. How can you torture the man so! Can't you see what you're doing, wracking the poor soul like this? Pulling him in little pieces all over again.

(There are sounds of assent from several CARDINALS.*)*

BERSTEIN   I think it would be in the best interest if we were to hear everything.

COURTLEIGH   Surely, My Lords, we have heard enough . . .

HADRIAN *(mounting the dais)*   But you shall hear more. They say that I gorged myself with sumptuous banquets at grand hotels. Once, after several days of starvation, I got a hard-earned begrudging and overdue fee from a magazine. I went and had an omelette at a small-town commercial doss-house which called itself "The Grand Hotel." They also say that, in my lodgings, I demanded elaborate dishes to be made from my own cookery book. Since I was beholden to my landlords I did indeed ask for special dishes —dishes of lentils and carrots—I do not touch meat—anything that was cheapest, cleanest, easiest and most filling. Each dish cost a few pence and I sometimes had one each day. And occasionally when I earned a little bit I spent a few shillings on apparatus conducive to personal cleanliness, soap, baths and so on. That is the story of my luxurious living, My Lords.

(There is a pause, and all keep silent.)

HADRIAN *(moving downstage and facing up)*   I have been provoked, abused, calumniated, traduced with insinuation, innuendo, misrepresentation, lies; my life has been held up to ridicule and most inferior contempt. I tell you this because, officially, I must correct an error. You may take it as an example of how your Catholics, laymen and clergy alike, can tire out and drive almost to death a man's body —perhaps even his soul. *(Moving upstage and turning)* But understand this, My Lords: by no words will I ever defend myself outside these walls. Nor do I speak in my own defence, Venerable Fathers, even to you. I, personally and of predilection, am indifferent to opinions, but it is your right to hear that which you have heard.

(There is another silence, then RAGNA *speaks out.)*

RAGNA *(waving the newspapers)* An enemy hath done this!

HADRIAN *(with candid delight)* Those are the first genuine words I have heard from Your Eminence's heart.

RAGNA *(in a voice of thunder)* Who is it has done this evil thing?

TALACRYN A reactionary blackmailer and a disappointed woman.

RAGNA *(roaring)* *Anathema sint:* Let them be smothered in the dunghill.

(Slowly, HADRIAN *picks up the Pontifical ring, places it on his finger, and sits.)*

HADRIAN *(in Pontifical manner)* Lord Cardinals, it is Our wish to be alone.

(The CARDINALS *exit up R and up L.* RAGNA *is the last to turn to go.)*

HADRIAN Lord Cardinal.

RAGNA *(turning and moving off the dais)* Holiness?

HADRIAN *(rising)* May We detain you a moment longer?

RAGNA Please, Holiness.

*(*HADRIAN *and* RAGNA *move downstage together,* RAGNA *to R.)*

HADRIAN *(with warmth and charm, in contrast to his earlier manner)* We are happy to think that Your Eminence is no longer opposed to Us.

RAGNA *(responding warmly)* I too am happy, Most Holy Father, that God has opened my eyes to the injustices done to Your Holiness. I beg that Your Holiness will forgive me for blindness in the past.

HADRIAN *(deceptively docile)* Your Eminence is already forgiven. We are particularly pleased to have your Lordship's co-operation at the present time since there is a matter particularly close to Our heart on which We would welcome your advice.

(During the following, HADRIAN *and* RAGNA *slowly circle the stage, behind the throne and down LC.)*

RAGNA Pray open Your heart, Most Holy Father.

HADRIAN   Very well. *(No bomb was ever dropped more gently.)* By way of emphasizing the essential difference between the Church Temporal—which We have already renounced—and the Church Apostolic, We have in mind to give away the Vatican Treasure.

RAGNA *(shaken)*   The Vatican Treasure! But has Your Holiness considered that most of the treasures are consecrated to the service of the Church?

HADRIAN   Yes. We have also considered that the Church exists for the service of God and His creatures. She does not serve either by keeping costly and beautiful things shut up in cupboards. Well, my Lord? Are you with Us or against us?

RAGNA *(after a pause)*   Holy Father, I am with You with all my heart. Under Your inspired guidance let the Church once more meet the world in the pure missionary spirit of Her greatest days. I shall follow whenever Your Holiness may lead.

HADRIAN   God bless Your Eminence for that. To tell the truth, I was in no mood for another fight.

(They both laugh.)

HADRIAN   Your Eminence, may I now suggest that you accompany Us to St. John Lateran?

RAGNA   *Va bene.* With great pleasure, Most Holy Father.

HADRIAN   They will be saying prayers there for those having authority in the Church. It would seem to be suitable occasion to celebrate our reconciliation.

RAGNA   *Benissimo*. Will Your Holiness go by carriage or in the *sedia gestatoria?*

HADRIAN   Perhaps Your Eminence is in the mood to indulge Our English eccentricities even further?

RAGNA *(falling into the trap)*   Your Holiness, with pleasure. *Of course.*

HADRIAN *(with a smile)*   Then we will walk.

RAGNA *(aghast)*   Walk! But, Holiness . . .

HADRIAN   Your Eminence did say you would follow wherever We may lead.

> *(He claps his hands.*
> FR. ROSE *enters up R.)*

HADRIAN   My sunshade, George. Cardinal Ragna is walking with us to Lateran.

> *(*FR. ROSE *exits.)*

RAGNA   But, Holy Father, the political situation is very, very dangerous.

> *(*FR. ROSE *enters, with the white, pontifical sunshade with its green lining.* HADRIAN *crosses and takes it from him.)*

HADRIAN *(smiling)*   Quite. But as We mentioned to Your Eminence once before . . .

RAGNA *(raising his hands to heaven)*   But, Holiness, I am too fat to become a martyr.

HADRIAN *(opening the sunshade)*   My Lord Cardinal, in every fat priest, there is always a bony martyr crying out for Beatitude.

> *(*HADRIAN *leads off up R, followed by the now faithful* RAGNA *crossing himself and tut-tutting, as the lights fade to a*
>
> BLACKOUT.*)*

SCENE SEVEN

The audience chamber.

Two chairs have been set RC and LC facing up towards the throne.

As the lights come up, a body of SWISS GUARDS *enters up R and take up their positions in an arc across the back of the stage. They are followed by two* CHAMBERLAINS *escorting* SANT *and* MRS. CROWE *from up L.* SANT *attempts a truculent nonchalance,* MRS. CROWE *is obviously nervous.*

The SENIOR CHAMBERLAIN *escorts them to the chairs,* SANT *to LC and* MRS. CROWE *RC, then both* CHAMBERLAINS *retire upstage.*

There is a silence in which SANT *and* MRS. CROWE *sit awkwardly facing a ring of implacable* SWITZERS.

MRS. CROWE (*in a stage whisper*) Oh dear, why don't they hurry up? Oh, I do wish I'd never come.

SANT (*also in a stage whisper*) Shut up, Nancy. Do you want them to hear you?

MRS. CROWE I just wish it was all over, that's all.

SANT   Can't you see that's just what he wants? He wants to get us rattled. But I'll rattle him first. *(He clinks the loose change in his pocket.)* Aye.

MRS. CROWE   Oh, I do hope you're right, Jerry.

SANT   Of course I am. You don't imagine I gave the papers all I know, do you? Not by a long chalk I didn't. Not by a very long chalk. He'll listen to me this time, or my name's not Jeremiah Sant.

> *(The* SWITZERS *come to attention.* HADRIAN *enters up R, followed by* TALACRYN, COURTLEIGH, *another* CARDINAL, *and* FR. ROSE. SANT *forgets himself and automatically makes to rise, then, remembering, sits down again insolently.*
>
>   HADRIAN *assumes the throne.* RAGNA *moves behind the throne L of it.* FR. ROSE *stands R of it and prepares to take notes on a clipboard.* TALACRYN *stands R of* ROSE, *and the other* CARDINALS *take up positions RC and LC.*
>
>   HADRIAN *makes a gesture dismissing the* SWISS GUARDS, *who, with the* CHAMBERLAINS, *exit up R.)*

HADRIAN   *(frigidly, but without menace)*   We have summoned you in order that ye may speak your minds to Us. But Our utterances and yours shall be recorded.

> *(He indicates* ROSE.*)*

SANT   I object. This was to be a private interview.

HADRIAN   In order to start in a conciliatory mood, We concede. *(To* MRS. CROWE*)* Madam, what do you want?

MRS. CROWE Well, you know why I came here. I—er—I— er . . . *(She looks desperately to* SANT *for a lead.)*

SANT I think it would be more advantageous to all parties if I was to speak for Mrs. Crowe.

HADRIAN We will concede this point also. Sir, we have received your questionable letter—are aware of your calumnies in the newspapers—and are now at a loss to know what more you could want of Us.

SANT *(rising)* Want? Well, I want reparation—damages, as you might say.

HADRIAN For what?

SANT Why, for the loss of time while I've had to be here, and for my business which I've been obliged to neglect while I've been kept waiting.

HADRIAN To what extent have you suffered?

SANT To what extent? *(Walking around below the throne)* Well, that shouldn't be difficult. I've been here since last July. Say eight months, and I generally allow a pound a day expenses. But it's cost me a sight more. You can add five hundred pounds for out-of-pockets. Then there's the business: say a year with salary and commission—call it three thousand. Then there's what we'll call damages *(significantly)* if you know what I mean. Well, including "damages" you might tot it all up together and call it— twenty thousand pounds.

HADRIAN And your companion?

SANT   Well, better say double it. Forty thousand pounds spot cash in sterling and we'll cry quits.

(HADRIAN *takes a quick look round upon his* CARDINALS, *who return it.*)

HADRIAN   You are demanding that We should pay you forty thousand pounds?

SANT *(sitting)*   That's correct.

HADRIAN   Why do you demand this sum of Us?

SANT   Why? I should have thought I'd made my meaning plain. Do you want bells on it?

MRS. CROWE *(obsequiously)*   Perhaps if I could have a private word with His Holiness . . .

HADRIAN   Daughter, your notorious conduct debars you from a private conversation with any clergyman except in the open confessional.

MRS. CROWE *(rising)*   Oh, I see! So it's like that, is it? Well, I think you're going to regret what you've just said. Mr. Sant was quite right about you. You must be shown up for what you really are. *(To* SANT, *as she sits)* Jerry, you tell him.

SANT *(To* MRS. CROWE: *gruffly)*   Now just take it easy, will you? And sit down. *(Rising, to* HADRIAN*)* I'm afraid the lady is a wee bit upset, as well she might be. And I expect she is a wee bit embarrassed by the presence of so many people. Could we not dispense with those fine-looking gentlemen *(pointing to the* CARDINALS*?)*

(He sits.)

HADRIAN *(to the* CARDINALS*)*   Your Eminences will be so good as to retire.

COURTLEIGH   Holiness, remember you are Sovereign within these walls.

RAGNA   I will tell the Chamberlains to take these people away.

HADRIAN   No. We thank your Lordships, but We are conducting this interview. Have no fears, since We have none.

(The CARDINALS *leave,* RAGNA *making gestures of despair.*
FR. ROSE *remains in the background.)*

HADRIAN   And now ...

SANT *(rising to L of the throne)*   Now, sir, I should like to make an end to this matter and I daresay you've other things to be getting on with yourself. Suppose you make a suggestion. I don't think you'll find us unreasonable.

HADRIAN *(with deceptive mildness)*   You ask that We should pay you forty thousand pounds—spot cash was the term you used—for damages which you say We have caused.

SANT   Aye, that's right.

HADRIAN   It's useless to point out to you that We did not ask you to waste your time in Rome?

SANT   In Rome! Not likely.

HADRIAN   And that We did not force you or induce you to neglect your business?

SANT *(getting angry)*   No! But I daresay you were banking on it that I'd never dare face you, weren't ye? If ye'd have had the civility to have answered my letters and made an appointment like I suggested a while back, we'd have had this settled and done with without all this unpleasantness.

> *(He sits again.)*

HADRIAN   For the credit of the human race, it must be said that indecent exhibitions of this kind are rare. But some men are gifted with an abnormal capacity for making fools of themselves. Mr. Sant, does it not occur to you that you are engaging in foolish and singularly dirty business?

SANT *(leaping up)*   Who d'ye think you're talking to? My hands are as clean as yours any day. Who skipped owing this lady here her rent, aye? Well, go on . . .

> *(HADRIAN turns to FR. ROSE. FR. ROSE produces a receipt from the papers on his board, and moves down to MRS. CROWE, who disdains it with a shrug. SANT snatches it.*
>
> FR. ROSE *returns upstage.)*

HADRIAN   You know, Madam, that We paid this bill the moment we were in a position to do so.

SANT Well, if you've paid her why shouldn't you pay me?

HADRIAN Because We owe you nothing.

SANT So that's the way of it, is it? Then, you'll be wanting to see a bit more about yer scabby little self in the papers then?

FR. ROSE Let me call the guard, Holiness.

HADRIAN *(signalling* FR. ROSE *to remain quiet)* Listen, Mr. Sant, We look upon you as a deeply injured man—

SANT *(sitting)* That's more like it.

HADRIAN —injured only by himself.

SANT What?

HADRIAN You have suffered loss and damage only because of your persistence in doing evil things. In this you have been your own enemy.

SANT *(rising)* Me own *what?* You sit there and tell me ...

HADRIAN *(raising his voice)* Mr. Sant, is it useless to ask you to change? You shall be helped. You will not be left alone.

SANT *(shouting)* I want what I come here to get—my money.

HADRIAN If you wish honestly to earn a better living, We shall give you that opportunity.

SANT   The hell with that. What about damages for the past?

HADRIAN *(rising)*   We promise you a chance for the future.

SANT *(with menace)*   You won't pay, then?

HADRIAN   On your terms—not one farthing. But We will help you to save your soul.

SANT *(almost out of his mind)*   You'll *save* my soul? You?

MRS. CROWE *(urgently)*   Jerry, sit down—please.

SANT *(to HADRIAN)*   You make me sick, you dirty Taigh.

MRS. CROWE *(rising: desperately)*   Jerry, I want to go. Please. It's no good.

SANT *(taking a step towards HADRIAN)*   He's just a little insect. Aren't ye?

MRS. CROWE   Jerry, please . . .

FR. ROSE *(running R in alarm)*   Guard! Presto! Presto!

SANT *(quite out of his mind, moving down LC and drawing a revolver)*   And ye know what to do with insects, don't ye? Tread them underfoot.

MRS. CROWE *(shrieking)*   Jerry!

> (SWISS GUARDS, *not knowing what is required of them, rush in shouting "Pronto! Pronto!")*

SANT   Vengeance is mine, saith the Lord! Halleluja!

(Before anyone can move, SANT *fires once.* HADRIAN *stands quite still.* FR. ROSE *rushes forward. The* GUARDS' *reactions are slower, but they follow.*

SANT *fires for the second time, and* MRS. CROWE *screams.* HADRIAN *remains still, though he seems to sway.*

As SANT *fires for the third time,* FR. ROSE *tries to interpose himself between* SANT *and* HADRIAN. *He fails, but manages to catch* HADRIAN *who now slowly subsides as a patch of crimson defiles the Apostolic whiteness of his robe.*

RAGNA, TALACRYN *and other* CARDINALS *rush in The* GUARDS *overpower* SANT, *half killing him and holding him on the floor. The* CARDINALS *surround the throne. All eyes are turned to* HADRIAN *who is supported by* TALACRYN *on one side and* RAGNA *on the other. The* GUARDS *fling* SANT *on his knees before the dying* POPE.)*

HADRIAN *(weakly)* Father, forgive them for they know not—*(he struggles for breath)*—what they . . . Venerable Fathers, Our will and pleasure is . . .

TALACRYN   Speak it, Most Holy Father.

HADRIAN   Venerable Fathers, We name you all the ministers of Our will. *(He turns towards* SANT.*)* Son, you are forgiven. You are free.

*(*SANT *is dragged off up L by the* GUARDS. *The hysterical* MRS. CROWE *exits with him.)*

HADRIAN   George, are you hurt? *(Unclasping his pectoral cross and giving it to* FR. ROSE*)* Dear Son, take this cross.

(FR. ROSE *takes the cross and backs away R, weeping.*
TALACRYN and RAGNA *now beckon the others to*
support HADRIAN'S *body and prepare to administer*
final absolution. The room fills with members of the
Sacred College and others.)

TALACRYN *(in a whisper: overcome with emotion)* The profession of faith, Most Holy Lord.

HADRIAN I believe all that which Holy Mother Church believes. I ask pardon of all men. Dear Jesus, be not to me a judge but a Saviour.

TALACRYN Saints of God, advance to help him: Angels of the Lord, come to meet him, receiving his soul, offering it in the Sight of the Most High.

(HADRIAN *indicates his wish to be raised to his feet.*
He slowly raises his right hand, which can hardly bear
the weight of the two huge Pontifical rings.)

HADRIAN May God Omnipotent, *(the sign of the cross)*
Father, *(the sign of the cross)* Son, *(the sign of the cross)*
and Holy Ghost, bless you.

(HADRIAN *dies. A bell begins a solemn toll. Four*
SWITZERS *lift up* HADRIAN'S *body and carry it slowly*
round the stage and off up L. As they do so, and the
CARDINALS *follow,* FR. ROSE *moves down C.*
    The lights gradually fade until only a spot is left
on him.)

FR. ROSE Prosit Quaesumus, Domine, animae famuli tui
Frederick William Rolfe, Hadriane, Summi Pontificis,

misericordiae tuae implorata clementia; ut ejus, in quo
speravit et creditit aeternum capiat, te miserante, con-
sortium. Per Dominum *(the sign of the cross).*

Yes, it had to happen. I suppose it was inevitable,
really . . . I don't suppose it has been given to every one
of you to have dissected a crab. But if you have, you will
have noted that under its hard shell there lies a labyrinth
of sensitive cells for the defence of which it is armed with
huge ferociously snapping claws.

In just such a manner, Frederick William Rolfe, hard
as adamant outside, was, within, the tenderest, the clev-
erest, the most unhappy, the most dreadful of all God's
creatures. Yet because he knew how strong he was, he
withstood the most fearful revilings and humiliations,
quite careless as to what the world might say. But faced
with the crass stupidity of the vulgar and obscene mob he
would cast aside his self-possession and the great crook-
edly-curving claws, once folded and still, would come
slashing and tearing with a violence that was sudden and
frightful.

But the One cannot stand forever against the Many
When the air filled with the impotent howls of all who
feared and therefore hated him, nothing was left in him
or of him, except the desire to feel the touch of sweet white
death.

And so it happened. So died Hadrian the Seventh,
Bishop, Servant of the servants of God, and maybe martyr.

ROLFE–FR. ROSE *(in unison)*   Let us pray for the repose of
his soul. He was so tired.

> *(As the end of the procession crosses,* ROLFE, *as he ap-
> peared at the beginning of Act One, walks on from up
> C and watches with approval the funeral cortege. He*

is smoking a cigarette and carries in his arms a huge
bundle of manuscript.
　　The remaining lights start to fade.)

ROLFE–FR. ROSE *(in unison)*　Let us pray for the repose of
his soul. He was so tired.

　　(The lights fade to a

　　　　BLACKOUT.*)*

SCENE EIGHT

ROLFE's *room in London as at the beginning of Act One.*
When the lights come up, ROLFE *enters clutching his bundle of manuscript and moves to the fireplace.*
There is a knock on the door.

ROLFE   Come in.

(MRS. CROWE *enters.*)

ROLFE   What do you want, Mrs. Crowe?

MRS. CROWE   I came up to tell you that there's the two men downstairs called to see you again.

(ROLFE *looks blank for a moment.*)

ROLFE   What?

MRS. CROWE (*with meaning*)   You know.

(ROLFE *pauses in thought for a second.*)

ROLFE (*eagerly*)   Oh yes, of course. Their Lordships. Show them up, please.

MRS. CROWE *(dubiously)* Very well, then.

> *(*MRS. CROWE *exits.*
> ROLFE *puts the manuscript on the chair C and
> tries to make himself look more respectable, then
> stands erect to receive his visitors.*
> *In a minute they enter. It is the two* BAILIFFS.
> *The younger holds a warrant of execution in his hand.
> The older smiles amiably.)*

1ST BAILIFF *(moving C)* Mr. Corvo?

ROLFE *(scarcely audible)* No.

1ST BAILIFF Sorry, sir, *Baron* Corvo.

ROLFE *(icily)* That is not my name.

1ST BAILIFF *(consulting his papers)* Of course, sir. You are
Mr. Frederick William Rolfe.

> *(*ROLFE *stands erect but one knee begins to tremble.
> The* BAILIFFS *look round the room, appraising its piti-
> ful contents with professional eyes.)*

1ST BAILIFF You were warned, Mr. Rolfe. I did warn you,
didn't I?

> *(*ROLFE *stands rigid, saying nothing.)*

1ST BAILIFF Now I am afraid we shall be obliged to distrain
your effects in accordance with this Warrant of Execution.

> *(Still* ROLFE *says nothing.)*

1ST BAILIFF   You do comprehend, don't you, Mr. Rolfe, that we are acting with the authority of a Warrant issued by the Court?

(ROLFE *still remains silent and immobile.*)

2ND BAILIFF   A Warrant of Execution ... *(He moves to the chair C.)* I'm afraid this'll have to go too, sir.

1ST BAILIFF *(looking suspiciously at the pile of manuscript)* What's this then? *Hadrian the Seventh.*

ROLFE *(picking up the manuscript and holding it to him)*   A book.

2ND BAILIFF *(piling books and all small items onto the chest-of-drawers)*   Write books, do you?

(He takes down the crucifix, the mirror and any other dressing and articles and puts them on the chest-of-drawers.
ROLFE *does not deign to answer.)*

1ST BAILIFF *(helping the other)*   What's it about then?

ROLFE   About? It's about a man who made the fatuous and frantic mistake of living before his time.

1ST BAILIFF   Any value?

(The SECOND BAILIFF *takes out the small chair and returns.)*

ROLFE   It's a masterpiece and, therefore, probably not worth tuppence.

(The two BAILIFFS *exchange glances of incomprehension.)*

ROLFE   At the same time, it is possibly beyond price. *(He passes his hands gently over the manuscript.)*

(The BAILIFFS *look more than ever confused.)*

1ST BAILIFF *(to his colleague)*   All right, then, let's get these out.

(The SECOND BAILIFF *takes out the C chair while the first moves the chest-of-drawers round. The* SECOND BAILIFF *re-enters and between them they take out the chest-of-drawers.*
    ROLFE *stands quite still, holding his manuscript.*
    After a moment the FIRST BAILIFF *returns, moves to* ROLFE, *takes the manuscript, and goes to the door.)*

1ST BAILIFF   Best not to take any chances, Mr. Rolfe. After all, you could be right.

(The FIRST BAILIFF *exits.*
    ROLFE *is left all alone in the bare room, standing rigidly as he has done from the moment the* BAILIFFS *came in. As he stands there, one knee begins to tremble violently.)*

CURTAIN

A NOTE ABOUT THE AUTHOR

Peter Luke was born in England in 1919 and grew up there and in Austria, Malta, and Palestine. After studying painting in London and Paris, he served in the Rifle Brigade during the Second World War. Thereafter he worked with a wine-shipping firm for nine years while writing plays and publishing stories and articles in periodicals, including *The New Statesman (& Nation)*, *The Cornhill,* and *Envoy.* He subsequently became book critic of *The Queen*, story editor for ABC Drama, and a play producer for the BBC. Two of his own plays—*Small Fish Are Sweet* and *Roll On, Bloomin' Death*—were staged at that time; several others appeared on television. In 1966–7 he directed *Them*, a film about the Sikh population of West London, and *Black Sound—Deep Song*, a film on Federico García Lorca commissioned by the BBC. Mr. Luke, his wife, and their five children now live in a remote region of Andalusia.

A NOTE ON THE TYPE

This book was set on the Linotype in Old Style No. 7. This face is largely based on a series originally cut by the Bruce Foundry in the early seventies, and that face, in its turn, appears to have followed in all essentials the details of a face designed and cut some years before by the celebrated Edinburgh type founders Miller and Richard. Old Style No. 7, composed in a page, gives a subdued color and an even texture that make it easily and comfortably read.